From Here

to *Maternity*

The Education

of a

Rookie Mom

Beth Teitell

From Here

to Maternity

Broadway Books / New York

PRINTED IN THE UNITED STATES OF AMERICA

BROADWAY BOOKS and its logo, a letter B bisected on the diagonal,
are trademarks of Random House, Inc.

Visit our website at www.broadwaybooks.com

First edition published 2005.

Book design by Donna Sinisgalli

Library of Congress Cataloging-in-Publication Data
Teitell, Beth.
From here to maternity : the education of a rookie mom /
Beth Teitell.
p. cm.
1. Motherhood. 2. Mothers. 3. Parents.
I. Title: Education of a rookie mom. II. Title.

HQ759.T442 2005
306.874'.3—dc22
2004054638

ISBN 0-7679-1694-8

1   3   5   7   9   10   8   6   4   2

For my sons

Contents

From Here

to Maternity

What I Never Expected When I Was Expecting: A Baby

$\mathcal{L}$ike so many women, when I first learned that I was pregnant my mind raced with important questions: Does a box of Milk Duds count as a serving of calcium? If I drink a Diet Coke when no one's looking, will it harm my baby? Where do the movie stars buy their maternity clothes, and is $95 way too much to spend on a cotton T-shirt if I'm not routinely—OK, ever—photographed by paparazzi?

I don't know if you'd call it mother's intuition, but somehow I knew these were not the issues to bring up with my obstetrician, who obsessed about fetal heartbeat and urine samples. So I cruised along on my own, doing the best I could, focusing not on my unborn child but on the real centerpiece of this scenario: me. *My* anti-stretch-mark strategies, *my* plans for a fulfilling maternity leave—I'd actually *read* some of the novels that I'd glibly discussed at book club (using Amazon's reader reviews as my guide)—and, of course, *my* cravings (which were really no different than the ones I'd been having since fourth grade, when my dieting career began).

So there I was, in my seventh month, accepting seats on the subway, flipping through Pottery Barn Kids catalogs, and basking in compliments about my "glow," when I made the mistake of going into a cute little boutique called Pregnancy and Beyond. And there, somewhere between the breast pumps and the nipple cream, it hit me: pregnancy is not an end unto itself. You don't get to be showered with gifts, throw tantrums, shop at Baby Gap, and basically act like a big baby yourself without, well . . . consequences.

In other words, the Beyond. And not some benign beyond, like at Bed Bath & Beyond, where the beyond means candles and potpourri. No, Pregnancy and Beyond is concerned with the ultimate beyond, the one that lasts a lifetime, that wakes up crying at 2 A.M.—and again at 3 A.M. and 4 A.M.—and then, in the blink of an eye, wants to borrow the car to drive to the tongue piercerie. And, if all the Parental Authorities offering advice were to be believed, this Beyond spelled the end of: spontaneous sex, premeditated sex, first-run movies, second-run movies, Chardonnay, Saks's 40-percent-off sales, string bikinis, and the freedom to own a white couch or anything white or, really, anything solid, silk, suede, or simply presentable.

My glow was fading. Fast. "Enjoy yourself now," the Authorities snickered as my due date neared. It was as if I'd been convicted of a crime and had but a few weeks left on the Outside before sentencing. But even as the Authorities were painting a picture of endless ear infections and dirty diapers, of a world without SundayStyles or *All Things Considered*, of life without brunch and naps (yours, not some kid's), they'd get this faraway look on their faces and smile. "Having kids is exhausting, stressful, lonely, bad for your career, your relationship, and your back—and expensive," a friend with an eighteen-month-old and a three-year-old confessed to me one day as she scrubbed crayon off her dining room wall while her children did battle in the background. But she and her husband were trying for a third, and my friend was considering staying home full-time. "I miss the kids when I'm away from them during the day," she told me. "They're great."

At that point she launched into some story about what a little genius her preschooler was—something having to do with a song he'd made up—but I wasn't listening. Four weeks away from having a child of my own, I was starting to ask some very basic questions, such as WHY COULDN'T I HAVE CONTENTED MYSELF WITH BEING AN AUNT? If parenthood was so great, I wanted to say to everyone, why were there so many disclaimers? Why all the remarks about how having kids is "an adjustment," and the little "jokes" about how mom's going "crazy"?

When I brought up this seeming contradiction to one of

my friends, she explained it this way: "Think of parenthood as the toughest job you'll ever love." An allusion to the Marines wasn't exactly what I wanted to hear, but what could I do? It was way too late to appeal the verdict. And so, partially to satisfy my curiosity, and partially because I was two weeks past my due date, I went ahead and had a child of my own, a baby boy who charmed me from the moment he was born, but who slept so little for the first few months of his life that I considered flinging myself in front of a minivan in hopes I'd end up in the hospital, where I could get some rest.

Is it like this for everyone? I wondered after a particularly long night of tears (his and mine). And if so, why had I not been warned? And yet, when I think about it rationally (possible only in retrospect), what could anyone have said? *"Psst. Don't have kids. You'll never exfoliate in peace again."* And even if someone had tried to tip me off, would I have listened? Probably not, since even as I was searching for a sleepaway child care center for my firstborn, my husband and I were expecting another baby. This time around—since I was already in the club—the Authorities weren't so cryptic, so brimming with the wonder of children. "You're braver than I am" was the standard response to the news of my second pregnancy.

I am not a brave person, so that was the last thing I wanted to hear, particularly from the very people who'd been asking me, almost from the moment I brought my first home from the hospital, when I was planning on having a second. It's like my life was a soap opera, and the audience was constantly demanding new plot developments. *OK, we get the idea that she's struggling with the one kid, let's throw in a second, and just to make it interesting, let's give her one of those side-by-side double strollers and see if she can fit through the door of a coffee shop.*

Who You Callin' Mama?

When I was figuring out what to call this book, I looked back on all the shameful things I'd done as a mother (not that I'm even close to hitting my stride). Ignorant of traditional lullabies, I'd sung my boys to sleep with a slow version of the *Brady Bunch* theme song. In a fit of greediness, I'd returned a Ralph Lauren layette outfit and used the store credit to buy myself a Kate Spade wallet. I'd mistaken a sheep for a goat at a petting zoo. I still can't make anything but a snake or a ball out of Play-Doh. The more I thought about it, the more I believed the title should be something honest, like *The World's Worst Mother Comes Clean.*

But then, in a rare moment of confidence—or, who knows, maybe it was simply the fear that such a title would open me up to litigation by my offspring—I realized that I'm not the world's worst mother. I'm just new at the game. And even though I have the familiarity with diaper-rash creams and the milk-stained couch to prove that I'm a parent, I'm still sort of surprised that I'm the mother of two people, both of whom look to me to make decisions for them—and very important decisions, too, beyond whether bow ties are too precious for little boys (yes). For example: I took my older son to the pediatrician's office for a flu shot, and the nurse asked if he'd had a shot last year. As someone who can't remember her own blood type, the date of her last period, or whether she's had the chicken pox, I had no idea. "Is the information by any chance in the chart?" I asked, peering over her shoulder. "I know I'm his mother, but . . ."

My shock over becoming a mother is just part of a larger imposter problem. I'm faking adulthood, too. My husband, Ken, and I met and married in nine months. Exactly nine months and two weeks after the caterers left, our first son was born. Then, just as I finished writing thank-you notes for all the kiddie yoga mats and Baby Einstein CDs, the second guy came along. As one of my friends said, noting how I'd gone from StairMaster queen to someone who gets her exercise pushing a Combi side to side, "It's like you're in the Witness Protection Program and you've been issued a new identity."

Was I prepared for this new me? I'd always assumed I'd have children, because like matching your purse to your shoes, it's what people do, and it's what I always wanted. But at the same time, I'd never baby-sat, changed a diaper, cooed at friends' babies, or really thought about how a baby would change my life (beyond the weight gain and nursery-decorating issues). I knew that Uma and Madonna had babies, and they seemed to get out a lot. I assumed I would, too—at least when I was able to tune out the scary stories from the Authorities. As Ken noted after the umpteenth warning: "Learning you're pregnant (the first time around) is like finding out that you have nine months to live, but that there will be an afterlife."

This book is the story of that afterlife—of life after birth—as experienced by me, a woman who never dreamed she'd use the word "playdate" or refer to herself in the third person. But just the other day, Mommy heard herself talking to her children, and Mommy was saying, "Mommy's going out now"—to stalk a sweater at Filene's Basement, but they didn't have to know that part—"and when Mommy gets home, Mommy and her two favorite boys are going over to Sam's house." For a *playdate*. It happens to the best of us, I guess.

And by "it" I mean the tendency to go gooey when talking about your children, or to swoon when you see a newborn's head, or to get choked up when you get a birth announcement from a friend. The other day a colleague on maternity leave brought her two-month-old into the *Boston Herald*, where I work as a lifestyle columnist. I was on deadline, but I rushed over to join the fawning crowd and practically yanked the infant out of her mother's arms. "It feels so good to hold a little baby," I said. (Mine, at ten months and twenty-four months, were no longer so tiny.)

Was that really me talking?

"I never thought this would happen to you," one of my colleagues said. She'd barely looked up from her *InStyle* during the baby show, and with her of-the-moment haircut and carefree lifestyle, she reminds me of the person I used to be, another lifetime ago. "Don't worry," I replied. "I'm still me."

This book is written by both of us: by the woman who still thinks of herself as a single career woman remotely observing all the baby madness, and by the mother hunting for a summer art class for her two little darlings. In other words, a person with an unpedicured foot in each world. So sit back, jump up, put a bottle on to warm, sit back, throw in some laundry, sit back, put the baby in the $75 must-have baby swing, sit back, take the baby out of the $75 must-have baby swing, sit back, jump up and walk around the living room bouncing the baby, sit back, try to make a phone call, hang up when the baby starts to cry, sit back, try on your pre-pregnancy jeans, cry yourself. Repeat. And enjoy.

Because as they say, motherhood's the toughest job you'll ever love.

Chapter 1

My Stroller, Myself

If there's one thing they drum into your head when your due date nears, it's this: you can't take your baby home from the hospital without a properly installed car seat. But as long as that's all set, the kid's yours, even if you prove irresponsible in more important ways, like forgetting to pack cute going-home outfits, or failing to finish the border you'd been stenciling in the nursery.

Since everyone makes such a production about the seat, even if you're the type who usually wings it—at my wedding I was writing place cards as my guests searched for their table assignments—this is one matter you take care of way before deadline.

Think how embarrassing it would be to be sent home sans bundle of joy. Friends, family, coworkers, and neighbors, all eager for a peek at the new baby, would be stopping by bearing gifts and lasagnas, and in your best *I Love Lucy* impersonation you'd have to bar them from the nursery, hustling them on their way before the absence of crying aroused suspicion. "The baby just fell asleep," you'd whisper, peeking into the empty bassinet and ushering the intruder toward the front door. "But really, thanks so much for coming."

Or . . . maybe you wouldn't go home empty-handed if you didn't have a car seat. Maybe you'd get to stay in the hospital with your baby. Think what a great scam that would be. That's where all the people who know how to bathe and diaper an infant are—and they work nights. If only I'd "forgotten" the car seat, to this day I'd still be living large, having meals prepared for me, my bed made by someone else. My only task would be periodically putting off the nurses and health-insurance auditors. "Should be anytime now," I'd say as I scanned the horizon, pretending to look for my long-lost car seat.

In the old days, there was no KGB nosing around the back of your car as you attempted to leave the hospital. The baby would ride home in the front seat, sleeping happily on Mom's lap as she lit a cigarette, exhaled some secondhand smoke, and swigged a mai tai from a thermos. Although this was arguably less safe for the kids, it did mean that Women on the Verge weren't sentenced to an afternoon of car seat selection and purchase.

Actually, it's not the car seat itself that's so problematic.

It's where it leads. Because many infant car seats are sold as "travel systems," the need to buy a car seat forced us to immediately confront the dizzying world of strollers. You know how every piece of furniture in your home is part of a network so intricate that the introduction of an ottoman in the living room can affect the decor of a room two floors away, and a bad couch bought right out of college can set up a chain reaction of color and fabric choices that will haunt you to your death bed? Well, the car seat has equally enormous ramifications.

With my due date looming, and my willingness to be seen in public diminishing, I realized we simply had to go shopping. Ken thought we should do a little research first. (Have I mentioned he's an emergency room doc—a pediatrician, no less?) So he read *Consumer Reports* for safety ratings, and I studied *People* and *US Weekly* to see what Hollywood mothers were pushing. Finally we were ready to make a purchase that was second in cost and importance only to our new home: baby's first stroller.

At the time, we thought it would be baby's only stroller, but that was before we learned that strollers are like shoes or bicycles. Specialized gear is required. You need one stroller nimble enough to maneuver through the aisles of the independent bookstore, a workhorse for the mall, a jogging stroller (but don't worry—as with running shoes, no actual jogging is required), a quick-folding stroller for the bus, so you're not set upon by an impatient public, and a formal stroller for weddings and bar mitzvahs. By the time our second son was a year old, Ken and I had amassed a fleet, and our vestibule looked like a parking lot. I'd become so obsessed with tot transportation that I'd wave to moms who happened to be pushing the same stroller I was, much the way Prius drivers acknowledge each other with a friendly toot.

In addition to a celebrity endorsement, I wanted a stroller that came in a fabric to complement a gorgeous red suede jacket I'd bought at the Loehmann's Grand Opening Sale in Boston, marked down from $1200 to $200. (Getting the stroller before the child, I didn't realize that a clashing pattern would be the least of the threats facing the garment, which succumbed to Similac stains before my son was four months old.)

Walking hand in hand into the baby store, Ken and I were more nervous than we would be several weeks later on our way over to Brigham and Women's Hospital to have our baby. Maybe it's because at the hospital we didn't really know what we were getting ourselves into, but in the store it was all too clear: we were poised to spend hundreds or thousands of dollars on enormous pieces of equipment and garish furnishings that would engulf our apartment, destroying what little decor we had—which was not quite Stickley, but *was* a step or two above Mickey.

We were assaulted by ExerSaucers festooned with every rattle and spinning toy known to marketing-kind, enormous swings that played tinny tunes, breast-feeding pillows in taxicab yellow, play mats with hanging octopuses, tartan baby seats. And their single unspoken message? As bad as this piece of equipment seems, *not* having it will be worse.

The baby stores should be required to provide on-site emotional counseling. Because beyond the obvious decorating challenges—how do you arrange furniture around the Fisher-Price Winnie the Pooh: 1, 2, 3 Exploring Tree?—lurk more serious issues that the baby merchandise brings to the surface.

It was at Babies "R" Us that one of my best friends, Dana, was forced to confront the kind of mother she was going to be (the rest of us had known for years): one who *might* go with the less expensive softer mattress—the increased risk of SIDS be damned—if it meant she could still go to the expensive highlights place. And a mom who preferred not to have a baby monitor. "If they'd sold white noise machines for the parents' room I would have taken one of *those*."

Dana told me she fled the store without making a single purchase. Almost every new mom I knew had similar stories. Soon-to-be urgently needed baby bottles, changing tables, cribs, all went unbought as expectant parents panicked about what lay ahead. Somehow—maybe it was Ken's years of medical training—we managed to buy what we needed on our first trip. Or perhaps we made it because we were lucky enough to get one of the store's nicer employees, a grandfatherly man (though not, it would emerge, an actual grandfather), who had come out of retirement to answer a calling to sell travel systems. Some people bond to a hairdresser, and come to believe that that person, and that person only, understands their bangs. We felt that Sol was the only person capable of understanding our baby's transportation needs, and we'd always call ahead to make sure he was on duty when the near-weekly need for subsequent purchases arose.

These included a playpen—excuse me—a play *yard*, which we bought despite intense societal pressure against caging children. We paid in cash, so there'd be no paper trail, and smuggled the yard into our apartment after everyone in the building had gone to bed. I wouldn't even own up to the purchase now, except that we returned it a week later because it threatened to fold up on our child.

Much later, we realized that Sol, well-intentioned as he was, had no idea what he was talking about. If he weren't so nice, I'd sue him for malpractice for letting us buy a two-ton travel system. But that first day, Ken and I thought we'd happened upon Dr. T. Berry Brazelton himself.

"What kind of stroller are you thinking of?" Sol asked as he walked us past wipe warmers, baby bathtubs, toy cell phones. Who knew such products existed? "Look at that," I said, pointing to the phone. Sol laughed. "They got all kinds of meshugena stuff now."

But it wasn't just the merchandise. The customers seemed a bit meshugena, too. "Can we register for gift certificates?" one father asked. A pregnant woman turned feral on her own mother when the expectant grandma suggested they look at Disney-themed bedding.

"It looks like a car showroom," Ken said when we arrived at our destination. There were sleek racing models, economy rides, sedans—all that was missing were infants draped seductively over the sun shades. Some strollers were so big I feared ownership would brand us as Stroller Utility Vehicle People. "Think what one of those would do to a Combi in a head-on collision," I said to Ken. "I wonder if any come with side-impact air bags?"

The threat to our reputation aside, we couldn't get one of the larger strollers. Even folded, they wouldn't fit in the trunk of our car and allow room for anything else. Unless we bought a minivan, or better yet an eighteen-wheeler, or moved closer to the store, many options were unworkable. My baby wasn't even born yet, and already doors were being closed.

"People like this one," Sol said, pointing at a Graco, the practical but unexciting Saturn of the stroller world. I gave it a push. "How does it feel?" Ken asked.

Unlike jeans, where I can tell with a glance that the thighs won't work, with the stroller I had no idea where to start. Would a fully reclining seat be important to me? Umbrella-style handles? Ball bearings? A toy bar? A foot brake? A beverage caddy? A retractable sunshade with UV-protected peek-a-boo window? Shock absorbers? A front-wheel steering system? A telescopic-folding aluminum chassis? Did I want an acoustic canopy with speakers for playing tapes or CDs to my child? Was I a pram person? Who could possibly know?

Sol showed us how to collapse the Graco, but I'd stopped paying attention. Amid the panicky couples I'd noticed a small group of very slim women, stylish in that Soho-meets-Greenwich way, one of them pregnant, though she barely looked it. They were gathered around a stroller that was commensurately attractive. "This is the one you want," one of the friends said with authority. When they walked away (to look at Petit Bateau clothing) I hustled over: for the first time in my life, I understood how men feel about Ferraris. I ran my hands over the Maclaren. It was, as I knew from my research, the stroller of the stars. Uma's baby rode in a $2,000 model, which, I learned, is upholstered in black leather so buttery a baby could sit naked in it. (Although of course you wouldn't let a drooling baby anywhere near it.) I pictured myself with the Maclaren, lunching in Hollywood with other stars and maybe a Miramax executive or two.

Could it be? Was I imbuing a Maclaren with the same transformative powers I usually credit to a brow wax? Actually lusting after a *stroller*? Yes.

This particular Maclaren cost almost $300—without a car seat. And yet, part of me thought the expense might be worth it. The Tiffany engagement ring of the stroller world, the Maclaren does your talking for you. "This is where we should splurge," I told Ken, "even if it means skimping on baby food."

But since we were poised to drop $175 on a high chair, we went with the Graco travel system. Like shoes that are comfortable in the store but turn cruel at home, the Graco seemed light enough in the showroom but became immovable once we set it up, which was no simple matter. It took us two hours and four smashed fingers to put it together. The instructions kept referring to various "tabs," and none appeared to exist. "Maybe we'd have better luck with a Japanese-language manual—is there one?" Ken asked as he struggled to insert what we had decided to designate as "tab A" into "tab B," while he pushed on what we figured must be "tab C." It would have been easier for him to reattach the limb of a child injured by the stroller than to install the wheels.

We told ourselves we could buy a new stroller anytime, yet the Graco hung in there, like a boyfriend you keep meaning to replace but never do. For the first year or so, whenever I saw a mother browsing calmly in a store while her child sat peacefully in some upscale brand, I'd think: *If I only had a designer ride, I could do that with my child.* In the grip of stroller envy, I believed that the right stroller was all that kept me from being able to poke around a bookstore with my kid (and then kids). I became so bold—so desperate—that I'd ambush parents on the street to find out what they were pushing, or shadow a nanny in an attempt to get a glimpse of the stroller's logo.

After a couple of years and many, many strollers, I realized the stroller wasn't my problem; it was me and my anxiety that my passengers might start to cry or need an emergency diaper change. And, unfortunately, stress is a problem even a $700 Bugaboo can't solve.

Chapter 2

Sleeping Like a Baby

There are two times in a woman's life when she's treated like a queen: when she's a bride (first wedding only), and when she's expecting (first pregnancy only). That's what Dana said when I told her I was having a baby. "Milk it," she advised. "After this, you're on your own."

So true, I thought to myself many months later, as I lay in the hospital bed, my reign having abruptly ended at 1:07 that morning. I was a few hours into the most comfortable sleep I'd had in months, when a nurse entered with a screaming baby. *Can't someone control that child?* Just as I was about to call the front desk to complain, the nurse said, "He was fussing in the nursery so we thought we should bring him in here."

I didn't want to be rude, but my room seemed like the worst place for a crying baby. If professional nurses couldn't staunch the wailing, what were my chances? They'd gone to school for that kind of thing. My total knowledge of newborns had been picked up at Baby Gap while buying presents for other people's babies: if you buy overalls and a little shirt, you should get the matching socks too, and maybe a cap, or you'll look cheap. Besides, weren't the nurses getting paid to care for him?

Yes, I had chosen to have a baby, but that didn't mean I wanted to start the full-blown mom thing right away. I wanted some time to settle in, to enjoy my status as a new mother without actually having to be one. I wanted a grace period, the way a new boss suggests you "observe for a few days, and then we'll get you started."

But the nurse positioned the baby—my baby—on my breast. "Let's get him latched on," she said. I looked down at my new son's dark little head of hair, and while I instantly loved him (as much as you can love someone whose politics and sense of humor are a mystery), I realized that this was not a person who understood that it's impolite to wake someone up at 4 A.M. I also knew—hoped?—that he and I were starting what would be a beautiful friendship, one that would blossom ideally between the hours of 9 A.M. and 7 P.M.

I'd seen babies in sitcoms and movies and commercials, so I knew what to expect when I took my new child home: he would cry, but not very often, and if he did "fuss" for more than ten minutes or so, a quick bounce on the knee or rock of the cradle would solve the problem. If he awoke at night, Ken and I could go into his room together to comfort him, and then look adoringly into each other's eyes as he fell immediately back to sleep while the two of us headed off for some canoodling.

Which brings me to: Day One at Home with Baby. Because Ken and I had Decided that having a baby Wasn't Going to Change Our Lives, the first thing we did when we returned to our condo was put our new baby in his travel system, schlep it down the stairs—where are the Sherpas when you really need them?—and go out for frozen yogurt. We spent the rest of the day congratulating ourselves for being such casual parents, and then around 10 P.M. we tucked the baby into the bassinet and lay down to go to (I can barely type the word, it seems so ludicrous now) sleep. A few seconds passed. *Hey, this motherhood thing isn't so hard after all*, I thought. *Maybe I'll have lots of children, and home-school them, and I'll continue to write for the newspaper, but I'll be a June Cleaver too, always baking cookies, and*—and that's when the rustling from the bassinet began, and . . . the crying started. Hey, our new roommate was making it hard to sleep.

"Maybe he's hungry," Ken said. I could tell by his voice that he was hoping hunger was the problem. In fact, he was promoting it as a theory, even when it seemed just as likely—to me—that a wet diaper might be the cause of the distress. But breast-feeding was in *my* job description, not Ken's, so as enlightened and as helpful as he is, he was hoping for an out. But did I have a right to complain? I mean,

I'm in bed with an actual pediatrician who can check for ear infections *at home*. What more could a woman want? I'll tell you. A dad who breast-feeds—at least at night.

Or, barring that, a baby who sleeps at night. Or during the day. We would have welcomed either. After a few weeks of almost constant wakefulness, day and night had no meaning beyond the TV schedule. Like a spy being tortured by prolonged exposure to bright lights, I'd lost all track of time, and I would have gladly revealed anything if it meant sleep, except that I had no information anyone could possibly want. Soon I started fantasizing about sleep—although not, for obvious reasons, dreaming about it.

Observers pitied me, yes, but I also detected skepticism. Whenever I told a new person about the long hours my child kept, I got the following response: "But he's got to sleep *sometime*."

"Tell *him* that," I'd say. But to be fair, my baby did weaken and allow himself a little shut-eye now and then— but only when he was in motion. Although I can't imagine any evolutionary advantage in this, he only slept while he was moving, preferably at fifty-five miles per hour, but he'd settle for less. So I'd walk the streets day and night, pushing my bundle of joy. I was Sisyphus, but instead of a rock I had a baby.

Like a shark, I had to keep going. Or else.

But you know how babies are: they use their cuteness to win people over, especially the elderly. The two of us would be out on the town (literally), and if I slowed down for a moment, to apply a Band-Aid to a new blister or to pop a No-Doz, the little old ladies would hustle over. "So peaceful," they'd coo as he breathed softly. "What a perfect angel."

A comment like that can push you over the edge, as can this advice, which I heard constantly: "You should sleep when he does." It's hard to stop yourself from striking the person who says it, but you must, since that person is almost always better rested than you, and will have the advantage in a fight. "Sounds good," I always wanted to respond, "but who will push me in a stroller while I push him?"

When it became clear that the sandman wasn't going to ride in and rescue me, I looked into getting a home treadmill, with the idea that I'd put the stroller on the machine, punch in a four-hour workout, and let him go for a nice long "walk." I was all set to have the equipment delivered when I remembered an accident at my gym where one of the treadmills malfunctioned, and the guy walking on it shot off the back like a cannonball.

How would I explain a high-speed crash to an ER doc—like my husband, for instance—or to the cop on duty at the station? The last thing I needed was to be slapped with a child-endangerment charge. Or was it? At least in the slammer I'd get some rest.

In the end, I decided against the treadmill. I didn't want some DA up for reelection perp-walking me into the courthouse, baby blanket over my head and mashed banana on my shoulder, a gaggle of well-groomed reporters goading me. "Hey, Treadmill Mom, is it true you haven't blow-dried your hair in four days?" "Treadmill Mom, when was the last time you read *The New Yorker*?"

At my low point—or, I should say, one of my low points—I wished (not really; yes, really) that my son would develop a cough so we could give him some medicine that caused—oh, it's too much to ask for—drowsiness. Even without a cough, I was pretty close to rationalizing a prophylactic dose of Benadryl during cold and flu season—for his own good. Everyone knows that a good night's sleep builds resistance!

Although, the way my luck was running, the Benadryl would probably knock him out for so long that I would panic, and end up force-feeding him a can of Jolt before the authorities got suspicious. I know it sounds crazy, but this very scenario almost happened to my friend Helen, despite her widely admired intelligence and common sense. Her baby liked to while away the day screaming her head off, and after six weeks this manner of passing time began to rattle Helen. One morning, when she was clinically insane from sleep deprivation—that's what she planned to tell the jury—she weakened and gave the baby a tiny drop of the gripe water that her well-meaning Jamaican neighbor had brought over as a gift.

It was as if she had shot the girl with a tranquilizer dart meant for an elephant. Where a moment ago the baby had been alive with agitation, she now lay limp in her mother's arms. "Wake her up!" Helen's husband yelled. "Wake her up!" The two of them were sure they'd done in their own child. They tried to rouse her. "Is she still breathing?" Daddy asked. She was! But hours went by, and all she did was . . . sleep. For the first time in a month and a half the apartment was quiet. They could have read. Or napped. Or smooched. If they hadn't been sick with fear and remorse. "All we wanted was for her to *start* crying," Helen told me later. What luck! That's exactly what happened. But once the girl woke up with no apparent ill effects, the question turned from which defense attorney to hire, to whether or not to use the gripe water again. Morally (meaning her position before becoming the mother of a colicky baby), Helen was opposed to pharmacological answers. But now that she saw that the gripe water worked, and that it wasn't toxic, and that she had some more in her possession, every day became a battle not to use it. It's sort of like opening a sealed tin of cookies you'd been saving for company: after eating just one, all bets are off. Eventually Helen had to throw the bottle away. "It was really hard," she said, over the familiar background crying.

Here's what I don't understand. Society always talks about how valuable its children are, and yet it allows the most vulnerable—the tiniest babies—to be cared for by people who are so mentally impaired they're no longer applying mascara or tracking sales at Banana Republic. We have studies proving that severe sleep deprivation slows a person's response time and clouds judgment, and yet in homes all over the country—split-level ranches with wall-to-wall, fourth-floor walkups, Victorians with original crown molding—mothers who themselves have developed colic are left alone with babies. No wonder an annoyance like Barney was able to get a foothold.

But I don't mean to cast those early sleepless months with my firstborn in a completely harsh light. A child who's up a lot during the night adds so much extra time to your day. Hours once wasted in slumber could be spent in productive thought, imagining your own premature death and how hard it will be on your sleepless darling, perhaps, or stressing about how the person filling in for you while you're on maternity leave is probably better at your job than you are—or were—and is more popular with your co-workers.

About 3 A.M. one night I tried to think of anything worse than having a child who doesn't sleep (in the realm of not-so-bad problems, of course, not in the grand scheme of things). I decided yes, there was one thing: being in a mothers' group with one of the cosmic lottery winners whose baby is a Good Sleeper. Remarks like "We had to wake her up at eight this morning" or "I set my alarm for two A.M. so I can check on him" can cause a rift that takes years to repair—say, not until your child gets into Harvard early admission and hers is skipping weekly meetings with his probation officer. And even that might not be enough.

My wakeup call came, well, constantly—but I realized the sleep-deprivation situation was completely out of control one night when I crawled from my son's room as if I were a Navy SEAL negotiating barbed wire, so desperate was I not to trigger the creaky floorboard that lurked like a land mine between his crib and the door. Why is it, I wondered, that an ambulance–fire truck convoy with all sirens blaring doesn't even register with him when he's outside; but indoors, someone two apartments away coughs and he's up for an hour?

Here's one theory: the kids are in cahoots with the baby sleep-aid manufacturers. Little Tyler and Alexis and Christopher get kickbacks for every drowse-inducing elixir sold. And it's a big market. Just as a woman desperate to erase *the appearance of fine lines and aging* will drop a hundred bucks on an ounce of hope, a parent with a bad sleeper on his or her hands will try anything . . . even the stuffed "Mommy Bear" (price: $59.95). It's an otherwise unremarkable teddy whose belly emits womb sounds. I didn't buy the bear so I can't say for sure that it doesn't lull children to sleep, but if it did, I have a feeling word would have spread. (Same as with diets and male hair-loss products.) Or maybe a bassinet that shakes and plays music is the answer, or a heating pad filled with cherry pits, or a mechanical swing, or a doll perfumed with "mom's scent." (Is it a deep nervous sweat?) And, of course, there are the CDs. *The Baby Soother* boasts that "91 percent of babies stopped crying when *The Baby Soother* was played *provided the baby heard the sounds within the first three months of life*." In other words, buy it on the way home from the hospital and start playing it immediately, just in case.

Our CD, *Stops Crying Guaranteed*, took reasonable children's songs like "London Bridge" and "Rock-a-Bye Baby," slowed them down, and overlaid a heartbeat. It claimed to be so effective that it carried a "do not operate heavy machinery while listening" warning. You should be so lucky to doze off and swerve into an oncoming Mack truck. Actually, they're right—you might fall asleep behind the wheel, but only because THE CD DOESN'T WORK and you will have been up all night.

There is one product I can imagine—a service, really—that would have worked: a baby bus. After finishing their routes for the day, Greyhound or city-owned buses could pick up bad sleepers all over town. Strapped into rear-facing car seats, the kids would be driven through the night in a special no-stopping lane. Boston to Jersey and back again, or maybe up toward Canada. The trip could start around 8 P.M., and then—let's make it 9 A.M. so Mom has time to work out and shower—the driver would deliver the tots back to their (now) loving parents.

If the insurance would be too high to make the "Babies on Board" bus economically feasible, or if no driver could handle that much pressure, how about a program that pairs infants with licensed insomniacs? The moms and dads would get some sleep; the babies would get to watch a lot of old Elizabeth Taylor and Joan Crawford movies; and after a night or two, I have a feeling the insomniacs would be cured. Or at least pretend they'd been.

Mad Mom Disease

I was on deadline at the *Herald*, inhaling Diet Coke and peanut M&M's, hoping a lead for my column would materialize, and wondering if maybe a bag of Baked Lays potato chips would help, or perhaps a trip to the ladies' room to reapply gloss, when my phone rang. To answer or not? My column was already half an hour late, and fifteen minutes had elapsed since I'd told my editor I was just "giving it one last read." Usually when my phone rings it's one of my friends, so from a professional standpoint picking up would not be smart. But what if my nanny was calling?

I grabbed the receiver. "I can't talk now, I'll have to call you back" was what I was planning to say, but if that was true, why did I pick up the phone? Before I had a chance to speak, I heard a newborn crying, and then my friend Allison's voice. "How long did you breast-feed?"

Allison's not what you'd call an earth mother (unless seaweed wraps and mud baths at Canyon Ranch count), and I could tell by her bathrobe and her dirty hair (audible over the phone) that she was not making idle chat. I knew that if I said "I only made it for six days" she would pack away her breasts and crack open a can of formula for her baby, and a Sam Adams for herself.

"How long did I breast-feed," I repeated, "or how long did I pretend to breast-feed?"

A loaded subject like breast-feeding can't be properly discussed on deadline—although here I'd picked up the phone and was apparently about to try.

I think Allison said her nipples were cracking, or maybe she said *she* was cracking. Physically I was in the *Herald* newsroom, amid the piles of dusty newspapers and barking city editors, but mentally I was back in the maternity hospital with my first son, trying without luck to get him to latch on to my breast, and wondering why something that was supposed to be so natural required a lactation consultant and a registered nurse—and that was after the pricey breast-feeding class I'd taken. I learned that breast-feeding could be painful and tricky, particularly at the beginning, but even so, the dominant picture in my mind reflected all the images I'd seen over the years of a mother lovingly holding her baby to her bosom as she nourished him with her own body, gazing down at his tiny head, projecting a supreme inner peace. In other words, the antithesis of the picture I was presenting to the assembled crew. I'd been breast-feeding for less than a day, and already my nipples felt like my feet did the only time I ever crammed them into a pair of stilettos. But at least when I decided to abandon the shoes, no one suggested I should keep trying until the searing pain disappeared. There were no podiatrists kneeling by my side, trying to fit my foot in just so, no studies showing the health benefits of four-inch heels and pointy toes, no Manolo League making me feel guilty for preferring flats.

As I tried to break the baby's suction with my finger so he could be removed from my breast without taking my nipple with him, I couldn't help but think how I'd chosen the wrong era to have a child. When my mother had me, not only was she knocked out for the birth—any discomfort would come months later, when she tried on her "skinny jeans" for the first time—but back then, breast-feeding was for peasants in distant countries and hippies. Now the PC pendulum has swung so far to the left that unless you have a doctor's note, you better be wearing a nursing bra.

I didn't need a lactation consultant and a maternity nurse, I needed an exit strategy. As luck would have it, I'd already developed two: Plan A, I show concern that I'm not making enough milk to nourish my baby, and the pediatrician insists I give my child formula. I'd put up a *small* fight. No need to mention my belief that true bonding was more likely to occur during a George Clooney movie or a nice Italian dinner. Wouldn't doing something we both enjoyed more likely foster feelings of love than an activity that left one person with bleeding nipples, and the other dangerously dehydrated?

"I'm not trying to be a pessimist," Helen had said when I mentioned this plan, "but what if you *do* make enough milk? What are you going to do then?"

"I'll call Dana," I said. The way the story went, Dana had gotten another friend out of breast-feeding simply by decreeing it didn't "suit" her, and sending the woman's husband out for Enfamil and Chardonnay. But for some crazy reason—maybe I wanted to do the best I could for my child, or maybe I was psyched about the cleavage—I knew that I should breast-feed. At least until I could concoct a decent excuse not to, that is. And if Plan A didn't work, I'd always have Plan B, which I'd unleash when my maternity leave ended.

From my hospital-bed vantage point, four months of breast-feeding seemed like a huge accomplishment, but not to the Nipple Nazis it didn't. When the lactation consultant asked me where I planned to pump at work, I explained that not only did I walk six miles round-trip to and from work each day (a walk that would be undoable with a nine-pound milking machine slung over my shoulder), but more important, I told her that I worked in a large, open newsroom, with no privacy whatsoever. To make my case, I mentioned that without even trying—without even feigning interest—I knew the most intimate personal details about the ten people who sit around me, and although they also knew all about me, I had to draw the line somewhere, and it would be at my engorged bosom. I assumed that would be the end of the discussion. The consultant seemed undaunted. "Just find a private place," she said. Had she never seen *All the President's Men? The Paper? Superman?*

I explained there are no private places—even the editor-in-chief's office has glass walls—but she was a problem solver. "What about the ladies' room?" she suggested brightly. When you work in a place where people take pride in the ink-stained mess, manufacturing and bottling food for an infant in the *bathroom* is not a good idea, particularly when the whole point is to make the baby *healthy*. I had the facts on my side, yet I was starting to feel like a real can't-do person, until I asked the consultant where *she* had pumped when *she'd* returned to work—at one of the largest maternity hospitals in the medical capital of the world, I might add. Her face clouded. "I couldn't find a place," she confided.

"Aha!" I wanted to yell, but I've found it's best not to rub someone's face in something when the potential rubee is the one deciding which sore breast to sic your newborn on next. And although this woman seemed perfectly nice, I sensed she wouldn't be so friendly if crossed. So instead of gloating, I returned to the challenge at hand.

Finally, working together, we got my son properly attached, and before leaving the hospital I even learned to do it myself. Although my milk didn't come in for two days— a period marked by feelings of worry, inadequacy, and wild optimism—things actually started to work. Well, from a nutritional point of view, at least. From a lifestyle perspective, they weren't working at all. Just before I had my baby I'd learned that newborns need to feed every two or three hours. That sounded alarmingly frequent, even to a grazer like me. Since I was not planning to breast-feed in public, I'd been worried about being on a short leash, but I'd had no idea just how short it would be. The babies negotiated themselves a great contract. Not only do they get to feed up to twelve times a day, but the clock starts ticking when the feeding begins, not when it ends, so if your child takes his time eating—and mine seemed to be part of the trendy "slow foods" movement—Mom has only a few minutes after coffee and dessert have been cleared before she has to start with the appetizers again.

Although I was frightened by the Medela pump I'd bought, once I saw what life was like feeding with only my breasts, I was desperate to get started with the machine—but I'd been warned against "introducing" the bottle too early lest I cause "nipple confusion." Nipple confusion, I learned, was a problem that arises when a child who's given a bottle to drink from finds it preferable to the breast. The first time I heard about nipple confusion a surge of hopefulness coursed through my aching, exhausted body. But, being the good mother I am, I waited the prescribed number of weeks, and then practically skipped to the closet to get my "Pump In Style." But when I unpacked it, and saw for the first time what exactly was involved, I didn't know if

I could go through with it. Sobbing, and feeling like a heifer with the maternal variant of Mad Cow—Mad Mom—I reminded myself that pumping equals *freedom* (and tried not to think of Janis Joplin's take on the word). I sterilized the tubes and the bottles and found an outlet near the TV so I could *try* to distract myself, and I got started. An ounce or two had dripped into each bottle when the baby started crying. He was hungry, was he? Well, I'll tell you one thing, he wasn't getting the pumped milk now, that was for sure. Those hard-earned drops of white gold were for Ken's 3 A.M. feeding. But uh-oh, my breasts were empty, and even if I decided to order my son a Domino's pizza, it wouldn't arrive for a half an hour. So I fed him the pumped milk. When his stomach was finally full, and I thought he could pay attention to important information, I explained that he was going to have to skip a meal or two to help me get ahead with the pumping. "It's for your own benefit," I said.

It seemed pretty obvious that I wasn't going to become one of those breast-feeding legends you hear about—a woman who makes presentations to the board of directors with her child discreetly nestled in a baby sling drinking, or the mother who does yoga or housework while nursing, or who makes so much milk that she pumps for friends' babies. At that point I was just hoping to avoid breast-feeding . . . incidents, I guess you'd call them. Dana, for example, had almost divorced her husband after he (or maybe his parents, she could never get it out of them) fed their daughter pumped milk when the baby wasn't even hungry.

"They must have wasted four or five ounces," she told me—years later, still furious. "Can you imagine how mad I was?"

I could, and it's enough to drive a woman to, well, *experiment* with formula. Not that I planned to, mind you, but one day, when our son was three weeks old and we were about to move from Ken's bachelor pad into an apartment large enough to accommodate an eight-pound baby and all of his paraphernalia, a sample of Similac arrived in the mail, like the Golden Ticket from *Charlie and the Chocolate Factory*.

"This will be for emergencies only," I told myself as I packed it into one of the kitchen boxes. And somehow I did manage to restrain myself for a few days. (OK, I couldn't find it for a while after we moved.) But then one day I was emptying the final moving box (exhausted but driven), and there it was! I pulled up a bar stool (a car seat, really), plunked my son down, wished him "*Salud!*" and poured him two fingers of Similac, neat.

Forget pumping—*this* was freedom. As he guzzled the new beverage on the menu—without so much as a "Hey, this tastes different"—I promised myself that I would only use the formula as a supplement. "Just to make sure he's getting enough to eat."

Do I need to tell you how quickly that sample disappeared? And do I need to tell you that every day—at least it seemed that frequent—there was news of yet another study showing the benefits of breast-feeding? I'd be opening a can

From Here to Maternity

of formula, telling myself "Just this one last time," when I'd hear a report on the radio saying that breast-fed kids were healthier, happier, better adjusted, and less likely to grow into adults who use the word "impact" as a verb.

Why was I upset if I was still breast-feeding? Well, by that point, the formula—the so-called "supplementation"—had become the main source of nutrition, and the breast milk, in turn, had become the supplement. Not that I confessed this generally. But I did tell Dana, because as you'd imagine, she's a great rationalizer. "It's like keeping kosher," she said. "There are different levels." We decided that on the Talmudic scale of breast-feeding I was neither Orthodox nor Conservative, but I still belonged to a temple. In other words, I was Reform. I'd never eat bacon ... at home.

And there was shame. While casual strangers would never think to inspect a baby bottle, the new moms with whom I was spending most of my time could tell with a mere sniff or a single glance that there was no mother's milk in that Avent bottle I was feeding my son. But I couldn't help myself. I was addicted, by proxy, to Similac.

Even so, something inside of me wouldn't let me give up breast-feeding entirely. Perhaps it was the daily 500-calorie bonus that breast-feeding mothers are promised, although I fear that number may be exaggerated. By the time you've dutifully consumed all the extra calcium and protein you need, you've spent the windfall.

I was thinking about the 500 calories, and how I'd like

to have the bonus working for me now, to offset the M&M's I'd been imbibing to help me finish my column, when I heard a voice coming from somewhere. *Oh right, Allison,* I thought. I'd forgotten the phone I was holding to my ear. "Thanks for your advice," she said tactfully, as the crying continued, "but I won't keep you any longer. I know you're on deadline."

Chapter 4

Working 9 to 5 (and 5 to 9)

*Y*ears ago, long before I would master—or even meet—the Diaper Genie, I worked for a chain of weekly newspapers in Greater Boston. One day I was assigned to drive around the state with Senator John Kerry on his "listening tour." At that point in my career—I had none to speak of—I thought that if I wrote one really good story I would be propelled, if not to dizzying heights, then at least to an altitude at which holding the handrail might be advisable. I hoped the Kerry piece would be my big break.

Unfortunately, nothing important happened that day. Or so I thought. In retrospect, I see that a life lesson had been presented before my very eyes. Two of Kerry's aides were in the car with us, and what struck me was that the sole determinant of the quality of their day was the senator's mood, which they discussed whenever he was out of earshot. And his importance was such that there was no need to use his name. It was always just "he" or "him," as in "I guess *he* didn't like the cookies." That comment came after we stopped at a convenience store to get a snack for *him*, and one of his aides went in to make the purchase but reemerged with the wrong kind. *He* wanted soft and chewy and the aide had gotten crunchy. Or vice versa.

"*He's* in a mood," one aide said to the other as the three of us watched *him* disappear into the quick mart.

As my friends had babies, and then one happened to me, I found myself thinking about those Kerry aides: the lack of control they appeared to wield over their own destinies, and their eagerness to please an all-powerful boss. And I recognized the day for what it was: a foreshadowing of my life as a mother. That's exactly how my friends and I act now. We judge the success of any outing by the mood-state of our little chief executive, referred to by pronoun only. "She was having fun, but then she got tired," or "It was too much for him."

And kids are terrible bosses. Mine are adorable, but they don't cut me a check at the end of the week. There's no annual performance review and absolutely no sick time or personal days—or personal minutes, even. When one of my supervisors is around, I can't talk on the phone, nap, or read. I do what any smart employee would, try to stay out of the boss's line of sight, but I always get sucked into new assignments anyway.

One day, when my first son was a few months old, I was

From Here to Maternity

thirty seconds into a five-minute mud mask when he decided he wanted a drink, stat. Apparently, the phrase "I don't get coffee" had gone right over his head during my new-employee orientation session. The mask, by the way, was part of a "new mom's de-stresser" kit given to me by someone who obviously had no children. Any woman who has ever worked for an infant would *know* that a large part of the new mom's stress comes precisely from not having time for mud masks, which is true even if the new mom has never been a mask person before. Post-baby, the mask becomes a symbol of all she can no longer do, and she comes to believe, truly believe, that she needs a mud mask. She wallows, if not in mud, at least in self-pity. But my stress—not to mention my pores—meant nothing to my son. It was time for him to eat.

When your work boss is unreasonably demanding, you can file a grievance with your union, or look for new work, or run crying to the ladies' room. But ask to speak to your home boss's supervisor? You'd be talking to yourself, sister. As for tendering your resignation or going home sick—equally unsatisfying. So what are you supposed to do? Whispering snide remarks behind the tiny tyrant's back is sort of satisfying, but it's more productive to recognize genius when you see it. As Dana explained when Helen was overwhelmed by her daughter's crying, "A baby's job is to cry." It may not look like it, but babies have mastered their profession.

Although it's never possible for me to remember that bit

of wisdom when one of my kids is enjoying a good long cry, I'll pass it on. Try to think of the kid not as your personal sleep terrorist, but as a workaholic who may someday earn enough to keep you up to your eyeballs in Kiehl's Rare-Earth Facial Cleansing Masques. Or think of him as a really good politician who always stays on message. And the message is: Baby.

You're probably familiar with the admonition not to pick a fight with someone who buys ink by the barrel. While I don't buy ink, I do write for a newspaper, and hence have more of a forum than my children. When my older son was a few months old, I showed him a copy of the paper with one of my columns in it. This wasn't meant to be threatening. I thought it only fair that he understood one of us would enjoy an advantage in putting forth her side of the story—not that I hoped it would come to that. But as usual he trumped me: never get in a fight with someone who has nothing to do all day but cry. *I* may need to grocery shop, or write thank-you notes, or GET OUTSIDE, but not him. Hey, he's only doing his job, and quite well, thank you very much.

Like many mothers, I'm often asked "Do you work outside the home?" I used to answer "Yes," but then I realized that wasn't quite true. It's only *inside* the home that I'm forced to work. Compared with what goes on at home at bath time, or mealtime, or anytime, my job as a newspaper columnist is a breeze. Let's compare:

If my editor is unhappy with my work, she sends a mes-

From Here to Maternity

sage over the in-house e-mail system or pokes her head out of her office and asks if I've "got a minute?" She'll express herself calmly, even if the presses are about to roll. If I'm on the phone, I finish up quickly*ish* and then saunter over and we'll discuss the matter in question *like adults*. I don't have to run into her office with food, then pick her up and fly her around the room cooing about all her wonderful qualities to calm her down. "What a cute editor! Who's the best editor in the whole world? Columnist loves her little editor." I don't pretend to gobble her feet, or clap her hands together. I don't speak in an insanely cheerful singsong voice that would make any reasonable person cringe. I don't plunk her in a vibrating seat, give her a bear with my scent, or blast a hideous version of "London Bridge Is Falling Down." Yes, I want my editor to like my work, but I'm not constantly selling it to her, as I am to my domestic board of directors. "Have some *nice* tortellini," I'll beg. "Who wants to take a *special* bath?" "Look at the present Mommy brought you!"

And if my editor is incontinent, it's her business, not mine. If she's up nights, I don't know about it.

And let's not even get into overtime. "Mommy was on the clock for twenty hours yesterday, so she's taking next Tuesday for herself." There's no explaining comp time to a two-month-old.

Let's look at the schedules of one employee who works outside the home and one who works inside:

9:20 A.M.: Toss off a quick apology for being late, explaining there was a long line at the dry cleaner's and you just had to pick up a dress you're planning to wear Saturday night. Settle in to discuss weekend plans with colleagues.

11:00 A.M.: Switch discussion to the subject of lunch.

11:30 A.M.: Do actual work for one whole hour—well, a whole hour minus the twenty-one minutes spent: in the bathroom; complaining to a coworker about how much the company expects of you; checking fares to Italy on the Internet; huddling in front of the building talking with the office smoker; trying to fix the copier so you could Xerox the *New Yorker* cartoon that shows a cat executive firing a dog employee ("Let's face it," the cat says from behind a big desk, "you and this organization have never been a good fit"). And minus two more minutes because you couldn't find a thumb tack to display your new artwork.

12:30 P.M.: Lunch.

2:30 P.M.: Complain that you ate too much for lunch and that now you feel fat. Vow to start diet tomorrow.

3 P.M.: Call best friend at her job. "Are you busy?" "No?" "Me neither. What are you doing later?"

4:45 P.M.: Solicit opinions on whether low-fat, low-carb, or some combo of the two, is the way to go.

5 P.M.: Call it a day. On the way home, stop by a wine bar to unwind.

INSIDE

6 A.M.: Rise, refreshed after thirty minutes of sleep, and dash into baby's room to turn off the human alarm clock. Pick up baby, bounce, feed, change diaper, change diaper again, change clothes, put in bouncy seat, remove from bouncy seat, try to stop the crying, wipe spit-up off new outfit, shake rattle, blow a raspberry into belly, play peek-a-boo, tickle some toes, change diaper.

6:15 A.M.: Repeat until 5 P.M. Repeat until 6 A.M. And so on.

After comparing these two itineraries I think we can all agree that the babies are the tougher bosses. But—and I hate to sound like a management apologist here—maybe it's not their fault. Maybe it's ours. After all, the adults are the ones writing the books the children all read, and yet none of them teach even the most fundamental leadership techniques. Where are the flap books that show a child how to motivate a burned-out staffer? Why no bath books like *Managing in Post-Partum Times* or *Getting to Yes?*

All of which is to say that my first maternity leave was

not the three-month vacation from work I'd been expecting. If you're unfamiliar with the way babies operate—as I was—you might think a maternity leave is like a very long paid holiday where you get to hang out with friends and park in the prime MOTHER WITH INFANT spots at the grocery store. A reason unto itself to have a child. A time to kick back, redo your kitchen, or get into great shape again.

Heading into my first leave I added *The Wall Street Journal* to our home-delivery list and scanned the apartment for home-improvement projects to initiate. The only interaction I had with *any* newspaper during those months was to carry it from the front stoop to the recycling bin. As for home improvement—I did the laundry when every drawer in the house was devoid of clothes and installed a fresh roll of toilet paper in the bathroom.

I don't want to sound like I'm not accepting responsibility, but I would have accomplished a lot more had my boss taken off some time himself, and maybe gone away on a singles weekend with some other babies, or a yoga retreat. Or he could have stayed on site, but developed a hobby or gotten some chores done. And it's not as if I didn't try to encourage him. We'd be sitting around our home office, frankly not getting that much done, apart from the crying, and I'd say, "Want to get an early start on spring cleaning?" He'd seem to indicate "yes," but instead of emptying his top drawer and deciding what he does and doesn't wear, he'd just lie there.

Even the most intractable visitor eventually picks up on

social cues. But when my son was a week old and I wanted a little time alone, I edged toward the door, sighed, and said, "Gosh, it's been so nice seeing you. We should do this again soon. Let's talk after the holidays." Did he pick up his fleece bunting and fumble around in his pockets for his primary-colored plastic car keys? Did he say "Next time at my crib?" No. He just stayed put.

But it's not just the babies that make a mom's job challenging. It's the other adults. "He needs a hat." "He shouldn't be wearing a hat." "He wants to be held." "He wants to be put down."

Did someone slap a 1-800-HOW'S MY MOTHERING? bumper sticker on my Graco travel system when I wasn't looking? I wondered after a particularly large number of random members of the public began volunteering advice. As a newspaper columnist I'm used to "constructive" feedback, but the *Herald* readers don't get to give it *as* I'm writing my column, and *not* to my face, either. I'm not typing away on deadline while a group of people I've never met stands looking over my shoulder saying: "The third graph drags." "The lead needs to be snappier." "Too many puns."

But when you're working as a mom, the feedback is nonstop, both from your boss, of course, and from shareholders you didn't even know you had. This was particularly true when I was on duty with my first son. Although it seems strange, he didn't always like to be held when he was crying. I'd be strolling him down the street, his cry clearing the sidewalks like an ambulance siren, and those unworried about hearing loss would come over. "You should pick him up." "He wants to be cuddled." "Try cradling him."

"I've tried," I used to call out as I ran by, speed being the only—potential—antidote. "It doesn't work."

The funny thing is that everyone thinks babies have it so easy. To travel with a baby is to hear the following sentiment repeated over and over: "That's the life, isn't it?" "But if being a baby is so great," I always want to respond, "why does he cry so much?" Then, the other day, as both of my home bosses wailed away despite my best efforts, I realized why babies often seem so miserable: it's lonely at the top.

Europe on 25 Diapers a Day

When my first son was two months old, for reasons I can no longer remember—maybe we were contestants on an Extreme Reality TV show?—Ken and I decided to take him leaf peeping in Vermont. When we told friends, many of whom were also living with tiny dictators, they were awed by our bravery.

These were people who in their professional lives coolly run emergency rooms and measure distant stars with radio telescopes. One wrote about the Mafia—cold-blooded killers who don't take kindly to bad press. Others routinely negotiated deals worth millions. And yet, when they heard about our plan to drive to Woodstock, the B&B capital of America, on paved roads, in a car rated tops in accident protection by *Consumer Reports*, with a pediatric emergency physician in attendance, the reaction was "Is it safe?" As if we'd announced we were going to sail solo across the Atlantic, or attempt Everest.

"Don't you have to train for years before doing something like that?" Helen asked. She wasn't trying to be a wet blanket—it's just that she was still shaken by our outing from a few days earlier. We'd decided it might be fun to go to Starbucks with our new babies. Pre-baby, neither of us went to Starbucks. We didn't like the coffee. But post-baby, Starbucks became a utopia: if we could just make it there, our loneliness and exhaustion would be gone. We'd be among real people, reading poetry or the *New York Times Arts & Leisure* section, while our babies dozed in their strollers or entertained themselves with a plastic lid.

We entered the store and our babies began their mournful duet. By the time our decafs were cool enough to drink, the glares from the Laptop People were more than we, in our weakened state, could handle. "I used to give people looks," Helen said, shouting above the din. "This must be payback." Aware that we had only a minute before a crowd wielding sharpened biscotti turned on us, we slapped the lids on our coffee cups and hit the road with our ear-splitting companions.

Our Vermont trip was to last about eight hours, which meant that if I hadn't already been on maternity leave, I would have had to use two vacation days in order just to pack. One thing they omit in the pre-baby parenting courses, but which immediately becomes the ruling force in your daily life, is that it takes X times 6 to prepare for any trip involving a baby, with X being the normal duration of the trip. What was once a ten-minute dash to the corner convenience store takes an hour to prep. Plus, it's not just the time, it's the fear factor. *She who forgets the wipes pays.*

With tension twisting my gut, I gathered provisions: two jumbo packages of Pampers (available in Vermont... but why risk it?); eight changes of clothing (I would have brought more, but space was tight—we could always stop at a Laundromat); a gross of pacifiers (these barrettes of the baby world lose themselves); a six-pack of Similac (my breast milk could suddenly dry up as we merged onto 91 North); enough Infant Motrin and Tylenol to medicate a day care center; the play mat with the educational hanging toys so our child wouldn't fall behind; a copy of *What to Expect the First Year*; and the Baby Bjorn carrier.

I brought the Bjorn even though our son wouldn't tolerate it. You've probably heard the line about second marriages—they're the triumph of hope over experience. The same was true of our relationship with the baby carrier. Walking around with him in it was like having a live grenade strapped to your chest, and yet we couldn't let go of the freedom the Bjorn promised. Wherever we looked, we'd see other babies cheerfully bopping along on their mom's or dad's chest. We'd be on some "family friendly" wilderness trail, grunting as we pushed our two-ton travel system over tree roots and rocks, when we'd be overtaken by another family, also with an infant—or maybe twin infants—except that those parents, instead of cursing balky wheels and doubting every choice they'd ever made in life, would be cruising along, discussing the latest movie they'd seen, or a good new restaurant in town, no more burdened than if they were toting an MP3 player. Ken and I would look at each other. "We really should give it another try, he's older now," one of us would say. Somehow he was never quite old enough, and then all of a sudden he was too old.

On the day of departure, a Diaper Genie protruded from the trunk and the baby swing clung to our roof rack. We looked like evacuees fleeing with everything we owned, or, to the trained eye, nervous urban parents—Nuppies— taking their first child on his first field trip. "We need a U-Haul," Ken said as he put his weight onto the trunk, almost cracking the Genie. "I can't believe I'm saying this," he added, "but I'm starting to understand why people buy minivans."

It was then that Ken hit upon his theory of the inverse relationship between the size of the infant and the mass and bulk of everything associated with the infant. "Young children are basically responsible for the increasing size of vehicles and the rising dependence on foreign oil," he noted. "Forty years ago, an infant was thrown into the front seat with its parent and no restraint whatsoever. Now you have to build an Apollo capsule in the back seat of your car." Thanks to car seats, a vehicle that used to hold six kids comfortably (three in the back seat, one riding between Mom and Dad in the front, and two bouncing around in the way back) now carries two.

We were finally ready to begin the Vermont assault when I thought I detected, although I was trying not to, a dirty diaper. "Do you smell something?" I asked. Subsequent experience has taught that 100 percent of the time when you think you smell something, you do, but because the action required to deal with the situation can disrupt an entire weekend, new parents always ask the question, in hopes that their partner will say "no." Actually, a single poorly timed dirty diaper can do more than throw off your schedule—it can drive a wedge between lifelong friends. In the time it takes to get your child out of his fancy French one-piece velour suit, install a new diaper, and resnap the outfit, the child will become hungry and the breast-feeding pillow will have to be unpacked from the bottom of the trunk. The feeding will create the need for another diaper change, and so on, until an entire day has passed, and the friends you were planning to visit have long since tired of your apologetic phone calls and no longer want to see you.

I think I've mentioned that at this point in his life, our son was happiest in a moving vehicle, so we loved highway driving, and if we could have found a house beside an on-ramp we would have bought it, resale value be damned. As you would imagine, the Vermont portion of our day-trip was filled with local roads, and it was at a particularly long red light that Ken, a board-certified pediatrician, developed his baby-friendly approach to stoplights: "the hiccup."

When word of the technique spread, new parents started calling night and day. I'd hear Ken on the phone, advising those suffering from pre-trip jitters. "You have to stop one hundred feet short of the stop line," he would begin, "and slowly accelerate in small bursts, never giving the impression the car has stopped, even for a moment.* The child is waiting for you to slip up, so the pressure is enormous and the consequences dire."

"Once the crying begins," he'd caution, "there is virtually no way to stop it. Simple acceleration will no longer treat the problem." For that reason, he'd always tell people that prevention is 90 percent of the cure. "When you're driving with an infant, the brakes should be used only to slow down, never to stop, unless you are ready to eject from the vehicle within seconds and you have baby-sitting support lined up."

Sometimes, although rarely, the parent on the other end of the line would still be grounded enough in reality to worry about public opinion, and would express concern that such a style of driving might elicit ridicule from other motorists. "It may be in your best interest to display a BABY ON BOARD placard," Ken would advise, "or to have a hand-sign you can hold up through the moon roof. Your car is no longer just transportation. It's a giant, combustion-powered pacifier."

We hiccupped our way to Woodstock, lucky enough to

---

* Speaking of not stopping, why isn't there a fighter-jet-style midair refueling service that would pull alongside your vehicle on the highway, and supply hungry and thirsty adults with needed snacks?

From Here to Maternity

not only hit the foliage at its peak, but to see enough cows, barns, and rusty antique tractors to fulfill our *lifetime* Vermont-scenery quota. Not that I could appreciate any of the rural charm I'd practically risked my life to get to. All I could focus on was my small charge and a few other babies I happened to notice, all of whom seemed to be disturbingly . . . calm.

(I've since developed two conflicting theories on those babies you see sitting placidly at the Four Seasons while their parents take tea: 1) Selection bias is at work—only the relaxed children are taken out for public display, so that while 100 percent of those you see out are "easy babies," they in fact represent only a small fraction of the actual infant population; all wailers are kept hidden at home. 2) Unbelievable as this may sound, your child may also appear calm to outsiders. As long as you're not the one under the baby's power, a little cry—or even a full-fledged tantrum—doesn't raise the Baby Alert Level to bright red.)

But, all in all, if you don't count the stress-induced neck cramp that plagued me for days, our first big outing as a family went very well, which was unfortunate, because it emboldened us to travel even farther, using modes of transportation that involved other people.

Innocent people.

I'm thinking in particular of a nice young man named Christopher, who had the misfortune to sit next to us on a Boston-to-Phoenix flight when our son was about ten months old. Ken had been invited to give a talk at a hospital there, and we thought it would be fun if we all went. Well, at least Ken and I thought it would be fun. The baby seemed to have other ideas. He started bawling the moment we lumbered onto the plane with the contents of our home. (Armies travel lighter.) But the flight itself was five hours, and when you consider that a delay of any length is possible, you realize that not only do you have to pack everything your child owns, but you must carry it on board with you, lest you not have access to it during the flight, and lest the airline lose it and you have to spend your entire vacation buying new clothes and equipment to schlep home. "Don't forget to put a name tag on the high chair in case they make us gate-check it," I told Ken as I tried to loop the Exer-Saucer over the stroller for easier carrying.

When I think back to flights of my youth, it seems that preboarding was a civil right. We used to visit relatives in Miami, and between the elderly snowbirds and the babies, the whole plane preboarded. It was an entitlement, like Social Security. And now, having paid into the system all these years, our generation's being shut out. These days, only the people who don't need to preboard—the business folks traveling light—get a head start. When they called our row, we made our way onto the narrow-bodied plane with the masses. I (accidentally) knocked out a few people who were already seated—I'd advise you not to swivel while wearing an enormous diaper bag over your shoulder. We caused a backup to the jetway entry while we tried to buckle the car seat into the airplane seat. I'd just finished stuffing my pump under the seat in front of me when, as I mentioned, my son started to cry. Christopher, who until now had been silent, looked up from his in-flight magazine. "I wish I could cry like that," he said, shaking his head. "Don't worry," I replied, "by the end of the trip you will be."

You know how they say having a child makes you look at the world in a different way? Before having children, I'd always assumed this meant that you'd become more concerned about the important things in life—deforestation and family and electing good leaders. But now I realize that when they say you "look" at the world in a different way, they mean it literally, as in you see things you never before noticed, never in a million years, such as uncovered electrical sockets and dangling phone cords. *What were they thinking?* I wondered as I surveyed our hotel room, not with my usual (i.e., childless) assessment—of the view, the hairdryer wattage, the minibar—but with an eye toward preventing grave bodily harm.

I would have loved to spray the room with a thick nontoxic foam that would have covered everything, but housekeeping frowns on that kind of thing, so I set about sticking in outlet covers I'd brought and taping soft pads on the corners of the coffee table and desk, and installing pinch guards on the closet and bathroom doors. I set up the hot pot (for sterilizing baby bottles) and unpacked my food grinder, and then I was finally ready to relax—*this was vacation.* As Dana pointed out, to travel with a young child is to realize that you may be away from work, but your job has come with you. She recalled a trip to Ireland she and her family took when her daughter was eighteen months old. "We were in a beautiful hotel that used to be a castle. There were these dramatic drapes and beautiful antique statuary, and we were drinking white wine and eating smoked salmon, and all Sarah wanted to do was to fling herself down the grand staircase. I was up and down every two seconds. Children have no sense of occasion."

Nor, at a certain age, do they understand that the DO NOT DISTURB sign means them or that it's a good idea, upon returning from vacation, to switch your inner clock back to your home time zone, or, most shockingly, that you buy an airplane seat so you can SIT in it. When our older son was twenty-two months old we went to Paris, and on the eight-hour flight home he (and Ken and I) got more exercise than an aerobics teacher gets in a week. Back to the bathroom, up to the first-class curtain, say hello to the friendly lady in 32C. Half the plane fell in love with our son as he made his rounds—but not the half that included the flight crew. Somewhere over the coast of Nova Scotia, during a face-off with the beverage cart, a steward looked at me and demanded, "Where do you want to go?" At that point I'd been walking for three hours. "*I* want to return to my seat," I replied, "but *he*"—gesturing to my son—"has other ideas."

Like many people on a long flight, I could no longer remember my life before the plane trip started, nor could I imagine that there would come a time when I *wouldn't* be on the plane, apologizing to other passengers as my son knocked into their food trays. After the fifth diaper change in the closet-sized bathroom, I decided we'd no longer travel farther than ten miles from home until the kids were old enough for college. And if for some reason we did have to go someplace distant, we'd simply move there—then, at least, we wouldn't have to travel back.

But somehow, almost before I knew it, we landed and then it was Monday morning and I had to report to work and file a column in just a few hours. I stared at my blank screen, looked up to see my editor heading toward me to ask about my piece, and I breathed a sigh of relief. Ahhhh. Finally some R&R.

Chapter 6

Let Them Eat Cake

I don't know as much about my heritage as I wish I did, but there's one thing of which I'm certain: I come from a long line of eaters. On my mother's side I'm descended from people who, in their day, broke the backs of buffets up and down the East Coast, from New York to Miami and back again. My grandmother once had to be helped from her girdle after getting her money's worth at a brunch. As a girl, my mom would sneak whole bars of Philadelphia cream cheese from the refrigerator—and that was years before she was on Atkins. You should see Aunt Eleanor work a jar of peanut butter. In the old photographs, my mom's aunts and female cousins are always shown turned to the side, in the thigh-slimming pose: front leg angled, toe pointed.

So naturally I expected that any child of mine would

have a healthy appetite. Well, if I hadn't watched the delivery room nurse attach my first son's ID bracelet with my own eyes, I'd doubt we were related, even distantly. Yes, he has my coloring, but three quarters of the world must have brown hair. He lacks the more telling trait: the "I'm just picking" gene, which allows a person to consume a quart of General Gao's Chicken leftovers while still believing she hasn't eaten a bite all day. "I don't know *why* I'm not losing weight."

Until my older son was twelve months old, he refused almost all food. Other than breast milk and formula, he would let virtually nothing with nutritive value pass his lips. Lovingly diced fresh fruit, mashed heirloom organic vegetables, free-range, antibiotic- and hormone-free chicken puréed in a food grinder that took hours to clean, all were received as attempts on his young life. "It's as if he thinks we're trying to poison him," Ken noted one evening after "dinner," as the two of us were—once again—forced to polish off our boy's untouched meal.

I think I mentioned that we dropped $175 on a fancy Italian high chair?

Sometimes, to toy with us, the kid would pretend to eat a Cheerio and then, just as Ken and I were high-fiving—*Yes! He's consumed three whole calories!*—and calling concerned relatives to report that the hunger strike had been broken, the Cheerio—gummed but still whole—would reemerge from his mouth and settle on his chin. Waiter, check please. The meal was over.

On good days, if I was lucky, he would allow himself to consume half a peeled grape, or a pinto bean picked out of a can of Progresso minestrone soup, or a single piece of Pirate's Booty.

OK, do you see how I just said if *I* was lucky? The child was the one facing starvation, but I was the one stressing out about it. In the world of self-help I think that's known as making someone else's problem your own, and the therapists advise against it. But deep down I feared that I was responsible for the situation. Because despite modeling very robust eating patterns in his presence, I wondered if, when he was in utero, I'd inadvertently passed on the message that food was bad. I've read that fetuses recognize the sound of their mother's voice very early on, which means he could have tuned in the time I left the Pea in the Pod maternity store crying because I looked "fat." Not five months pregnant. Fat.

And that was just the beginning. Looking back, I realize that he must have been listening in during the contentious weight-related negotiations at my OB's office. He would have heard me trying to convince the weigh-in officer to round down from 144 to 140, or frantically trying to determine how many calories I'd be wasting on the sugary orange beverage they make you drink for the glucose-tolerance test, and then inquiring as to whether I could substitute an equally fattening food of my choosing, like a Snickers bar. "No one's ever asked us that before," the nurse told me, denying my request. "Never?" I responded. "What's wrong with people?"

And he was also on-site when Ken suggested I take a lesson from wrestlers and hit the steam room before an OB appointment to sweat off a few pounds. Ken was joking, but humor's a subtle thing, and between the uterine walls and all that amniotic fluid, maybe the baby didn't get it.

Or perhaps my son's interest in dieting started when he arrived. A recent study warned that even infants can be affected by seeing violence on television. I've always been careful about having the news on when my kids are in the room—although I fear that PBS's Caillou, a four-year-old cartoon character, with his foot stomping and whiny behavior, may be more harmful than the most sensationalized program—but after reading about the dangers of secondhand TV I realized that magazines and catalogs might also pose a heretofore unrecognized threat to young minds. Maybe I'd mistakenly left out the *New Yorker* cartoon headlined "It begins." It shows an infant sitting in front of a mirror thinking, "This diaper makes my butt look big." Or perhaps one day when I wasn't paying attention, my son flipped through the Hanna Andersson catalog, noticed all the unflattering horizontal stripes, and panicked. "Uh-oh," he probably thought, "I know she loves this stuff—she gives it as gifts all the time—I better do something about these folds in my thighs."

While relatives worried about my son's eating habits, or

lack thereof, and spent their days trying to think of foods he might like, I was on a different mission: I wanted to learn his secret. The way I figured it, in just a few months he'd managed to master the very activity I'd been working at for decades.

"How do you do it?" I'd coo as I rocked him to sleep at night. "What's your trick?" I'd ask as I tickled his feet. I pretended it was all fun and games, but I'd never been so goal-oriented in my entire life.

He didn't say much; like the best teachers, he taught by example. His most instructive lessons often came at the pediatrician's office. We'd be there for a routine healthy-baby checkup, and it would emerge that while he was in the 95th percentile for height, he was only in the 75th for weight. If that had been me, I would have hit the lobby pharmacy for M&M's and then stopped on the way home for a celebratory frozen yogurt, but not him. The kid stayed focused.

I probably didn't take his eating "problem" as seriously as I should've. I don't think I was physically capable of worrying about someone eating too little. In my mind it was like having too many built-in bookcases, or too many accrued airline miles.

And there was an additional issue. Like a gradual weight gain that sneaks up on you until you're down to one pair of forgiving pants and a stretchy skirt, the gravity of the situation wasn't immediately apparent. For the first few months, of course, he wasn't even supposed to eat food, so we had no way of knowing what or who we were dealing with. But then one day, when I was flipping through *What to Expect the First Year* (so I could take pleasure in the milestones my four-month-old genius had passed ahead of schedule), I came upon this shocking title: "Thinking About Solids." Solids? "Thinking About Seeing a Movie in a Theater" would have been more on the mark, or "Thinking About Going Out Spontaneously."

But at least there was some wiggle room. While the good mother was supposed to *think* about solids at four months, the message I chose to take from *What to Expect* was that Mom didn't really have to take action until the fifth month, which seemed really far away at the time.

Even though I had weeks to go before the *What to Expect* deadline, as a show of good faith I went out, bought solids, and attempted an introduction. Because I'd read that it can take a few tries for the child to get the hang of eating, I wasn't worried when he rejected my offerings. Just as I continue to do sit-ups in the belief that someday I'll see results, I kept trying to make the sale. *Baby, peas, peas, baby*. But their relationship was going nowhere. I probably wouldn't have thought too much about it, beyond being jealous of his willpower, except that reports of other babies eating started to trickle in. I'd return from a playdate in a down mood and when Ken asked what was wrong, I'd say, "Caroline loves apricots" or "Tim eats rice cereal. And carrots."

And day by day the situation got worse. Friends who came to visit with their babies started bringing along Tupperware containers of mashed vegetables or puréed chicken, and as they bibbed their child and took out a favored Winnie the Pooh spoon, Ken or I would slink over to the Similac cabinet and pour our son his lunch—as if he were on a liquid meal-replacement plan.

Worse than our friends, though, were the mothers I'd encounter at various Mommy and Me classes, or in the playground. Eating, I've learned, is a competitive sport. Later, these parents will be bragging about their kids' soccer talent, or the job at the big law firm, or the weekly visits to the assisted living facility, but during that first year, the ability to enjoy edamame was the stuff of pride.

"Julia eats everything," one mom told me as we pushed our kids on the swings at the park. "Avocado rolls, broccoli, vegetable pâté. And she just loves Thai. What are your guy's favorites?"

"Herring," I lied. "He loves it."

"Oh," she said, "I wonder if Julia would like that, too. We've never thought of serving it to her. But what a great source of protein."

Protein, schmotein. By that point I was less concerned about malnutrition than image. So I went to the bookstore and bought some guides that promised to turn my little boy into someone who could hold his own at my mom's family reunions. Ken and I, and the rest of our son's dedicated staff, tried everything: "Open the hangar, here comes the airplane." "Oh, look, a choo-choo train is pulling into the station." "There goes Mr. Rabbit hopping into his hole." But our boy was no fool. He saw what we were up to, and it strengthened his resolve.

"Look at it this way," Dana said, trying to console me, "you've got one less person to cook for." And, she added, no peas or carrots meant no stained onesies.

It was something, I guess.

But the medical establishment eventually caught up with us. At my son's one-year doctor's appointment, under bright lights and weakened from spending forty-five minutes in the waiting room struggling to keep him away from a sneezing toddler, I admitted that my son's daily diet consisted of five nine-ounce bottles of Similac. I'd been living a lie for so long that it felt good to come clean, even though the pediatrician laid down the law: Switch off formula and onto milk, cut down to two bottles a day, and in hunger, he explained, my boy would turn to food.

"Yes, yes, of course." And I meant it. But then, when we got outside the doctor's office, my son started to melt down. Looking around furtively, like someone about to make a drug drop, I reached into the stroller storage pocket, grabbed a can of Similac, and poured it into the bottle. Knowing that he'd be happily occupied for a few minutes, I pulled out a Diet Coke—*my* Similac—and called Ken. "I've become an enabler," I said. "I see how it happens to people. There are reasons you want someone to drink."

But codependent as I was, I knew this little party had to end. I thought of a brilliant idea, although I never actually tried it. While my son wouldn't eat what you and I consider "food," he *was* quite eager to sample a cuisine of gravel, chewed gum, acorns, screws, and other such delicacies. Anything that had been blessed by the floor, or even better the ground outside, was also tempting. So why not trick him into eating by making him think he was getting away with forbidden foods? If he thought he was putting one over on me, his gustatory juices might just flow.

My fantasy plan was to stock a just-cleaned floor with carrots and bananas, and then, as he approached, I'd yell, "Not for eating—just for looking!" What if I disguised hummus as wet sand, and sliced cucumbers to resemble coins? He'd happily stuff that "food" into his face. I mentioned the idea to my mom; she didn't find it funny. "But if you teach him to eat off the floor, how will he understand that it's not really OK?"

I decided not to explain the so-called five-second rule. If food or a pacifier falls on the floor, and you don't have or are too tired to fetch a replacement, you're within your rights to hand it back to the child if you snatch it off the floor before five seconds have elapsed. (The time limit can be increased to five minutes if the drop wasn't observed by another adult, or if the item in question doesn't fall "face"-first.)

I never fed my son off the floor—not in a premeditated way—yet to this day, some three years after he and solids made a wary acquaintance, the relationship is not what you'd call stable. As I watched other children eat all manner of foods served to them by their parents, I used to wonder what was wrong with my cooking skills—that is, until I had a second child, and he became old enough for solids. I duti-fully brought out the jarred baby food and cereals, but I expected nothing, like a lab rat suffering from learned help-lessness.

But wait! Was that a baby's mouth opening for a little rubber-tipped spoon filled with rice cereal? Yes it was! "Get the yellow squash!" I called out to Ken, as our boy worked his way through a jar of green beans. "And get the video camera."

"Who wants more sweet potatoes?" I asked, as Ken zoomed in.

I could barely believe it. Finally, I was the mom taking out the ziplock baggie filled with pretzel sticks. I was the mom cutting my own food into tiny pieces for my eager child, and whipping out the bib. And I couldn't have been happier.

Or could I?

A small but *growing* doubt started to nag. What if he takes after my side of the family?

Chapter 7

The Itsy-Bitsy What Do You Call It?

Was I imagining it, or was he giving me a Look?

It was a Sunday afternoon in early spring, and my older son and I were in the dreaded Water Babies class. I would have been willing to let my child, beloved as he was, go through life as a landlubber if it meant I didn't have to stand chest-high in a freezing pool for forty-five minutes every weekend. Ken, however, thought learning to feel comfortable in the water would be beneficial, and since it was hard to make a convincing anti-swim argument, I signed him up. "But what about chlorine hazards?" I asked weakly.

Like a dental checkup that consists of a painful cleaning and a stern flossing lecture, yet turns up no cavities, the swim class had been going as well as could be expected.

Then, out of nowhere, the teacher sprung a pop quiz on us—*paying* customers, I felt like reminding her.

"OK, mommies and daddies," she said, "now we're going to sing 'Pop Goes the Weasel' and swirl the kids around."

The other parents started in—a bit smugly, to my ear, and not just with the chorus, either: "All around the cobbler's bench/The monkey chased the weasel/The monkey thought it was all in fun/But pop goes the weasel!" But then, as I was about to repeat what we'd just sung, they continued: "A penny for a spool of thread/A penny for a needle/That's the way the money goes/Pop goes the weasel!"

A spool of thread? A needle? More verses? Who remembered? Not me, that was for sure. But my child was staring at me expecting more, more, more. The options flashed past . . .

1) I could pretend to drown. Compared with dying, ignorance of a few lyrics would seem like nothing. (The eulogy wouldn't even have mentioned it.) But going under posed serious logistical problems, both for my hair (in case some idiot resuscitated me) and for my son's survival.

2) I could mouth the words as I used to do at birthday parties, when I actually knew the lyrics to the "Happy Birthday" song but was too embarrassed about my off-key voice to sing. I would have gone with this option, but two sets of video-

taping grandparents happened to be observing that day, and I feared that I, Milli Vanilli, would become that stranger in their home movies that everyone would laugh at for generations.

3) I could make up in enthusiasm what I lack in knowledge, which is how I handle similar situations in the nonpediatric part of my life.

Number 3 held the most promise. I swished my son around with extra vigor and even allowed my hair to get wet for an especially good "POP! goes the weasel," which I shouted as I sprung out of the water. "Did you see that?" I asked my son. "Did you see how big Mommy popped?"

That's when he flashed me the Look. It was the world-weary teenager's "Mom, you're embarrassing me" glare you expect when you drop your son off at the mall, not from a person wearing a double swim diaper. Had my substandard performance driven him to a state of precocious parental disgust? Child psychologists haven't studied nursery-rhyme disappointment in preverbal subjects, but according to my own research, a ten-month-old can recognize when his mother's on the wrong side of the bell curve.

"Did you notice how Mommy popped so well?" I repeated. He didn't answer. Maybe he was too cold to speak. That was it. Or he was trying to pretend he didn't know me.

"I wish Daddy were in the pool," I said, and not just because his presence would have meant that I could have been elsewhere. I was pretty sure Ken wouldn't have known the words either. Just thinking about *his* ignorance made me feel better. If a pediatrician doesn't know about some obscure needle and thread, a civilian can't be expected to.

In fact, I was almost certain Ken wouldn't know the words because it had emerged recently that neither of us knew what the baker does after the "pat it and roll it" business in the "Pat-a-Cake, Pat-a-Cake" rhyme.

"The world is divided into people who know what happens after the rolling and those who don't," Ken said one morning, after our sorry attempt to entertain our little boy. Eager to do the best for our son, we started mumbling some words, but the two of us sounded like the monster in *Young Frankenstein*, who lumbers onstage in black tie and top hat, incomprehensibly bleating the words to "Puttin' on the Ritz."

I let my baby's Look pass without comment. But even so, on the way home from class I couldn't help but point out what a Lucky Boy he was to be learning to swim, and how his bathing suit cost more than mine. (No need to mention that the steep cost was my fault—the price I paid for shopping at a fancy boutique instead of bargain hunting on the Internet.)

My remarks fell on deaf ears. He'd fallen asleep. Alone with my thoughts, I realized that, in a way, this was the unmasking I'd been dreading for years. Even before having children, I'd worried that when I did have a child someday, he'd ask me a question, in public, to which I didn't know the answer. I didn't care about "Where does the Tooth Fairy live?" or even the awkward "How are babies made?" I was stressed about the things I *should* be able to explain: "How does a plane fly?" "What led to the demise of the Ottoman Empire?"

Kids may look cute, but they're little devils. They never pop the tricky ones in the privacy of your own home, where you can answer, "Have you brushed your teeth yet, young man?" No, they wait until there are witnesses to interrogate you, and no diversionary tactics are available. Which is why, no matter how tempting it may be, I've decided never to bring my boys to the *Herald* newsroom on Take Our Children to Work Day. I can already see it. "Sweetheart, this is our city editor." "Mommy, who's fifth in line to succeed the President, the Secretary of the Treasury or the Secretary of Defense?"

Still, as worried as I was about being revealed as an ignoramus, I always figured such public humiliation was years off. "Mommy, what led the painters of the Boston School to turn their backs on Modernism?" That day in the swim class my boy was only ten months old—he wasn't even close to talking, let alone making humiliating inquiries—"Mommy, how does the Federal Reserve implement monetary policy?" So I assumed I had plenty of time to bone up on basic facts, to memorize, once and for all, the Earth's age, the whole gravity thing, the definition of a quark.

But incredibly, I was already too late. As if there isn't enough to contend with as a new mother, it turns out you're supposed to know the words to a seemingly endless play list of kiddie songs and nursery rhymes.

Is there a *Complete Idiot's Guide to Mother Goose?*

When I was honest with myself, and I saw no need to be often, I admitted that this singing issue had been building; it's just that this little episode happened to be public. In fact, night after night, when my son and I were alone in his darkened room, I was trying to hide my shortcoming. Instead of singing "boring" lullabies—i.e., lullabies whose lyrics were a mystery to me—I'd sing songs such as the theme from *The Brady Bunch*, which I knew entirely.

I'd convinced myself that my little substitutions were harmless. Beneficial even. Isn't a song about a loving blended family more soothing than one about a treetop cradle that's poised to plummet?

But I knew I was rationalizing. *You need to talk to someone*, I told myself. I briefly considered calling one of those anonymous parental stress hotlines and whispering into the phone: "I don't know why the cheese ends up alone in 'The Farmer and the Dell.' " But I realized I didn't want to confess something unspeakable to a stranger. For all I knew, she'd be Maria von Trapp, incapable of understanding a woman who didn't travel with a guitar and make up songs about her favorite things whenever she felt sad, and I'd end up feeling sadder than before—and with no guitar to console me.

No, it was better to talk to someone who would validate my ignorance, so I called Allison, a woman who will staple a hem if time is tight—and then leave the staple in for the lifetime of the garment. "Do you, uh, ever feel that there are *a lot* of songs we're expected to know?"

"For a long time, I didn't know the words to 'Head, Shoulders, Knees and Toes,' " she confessed. "People ask me how that's *possible*. Well, I never baby-sat or spent any time around kids."

"Hey!" I thought happily. "*No one* knows any lyrics." But that's not true, or my embarrassment in the pool that Sunday afternoon would never have occurred. No, I'm simply drawn to the lyrically challenged.

Except for my friend Holly. I like her despite the fact that she makes up songs (not to cover ignorance). We were at the playground recently, and when she nicely started pushing my son on the swing, she—not nicely—let loose with a song about . . . swinging.

"Swinging, swinging down at the playground," she sang, to the tune of "Bicycle Built for Two."

"Swinging, swinging and looking all around
I love looking at the sky
But Mom don't push too high
Because I look sweet
Upon a seat
Of a swing that is just my size."

As she crooned the chorus, I decided to enumerate the *other* talents I could pass on to my children (but what those might be escaped me momentarily). I tried to console myself with the thought that maybe lyrics to all those songs are taught at *some* prenatal classes, just not at ours. Our nurse-instructor had focused on breathing through the contractions, at what point in your labor to come to the hospital, and what happens if you need a C-section. Trivial matters, none of which I paid attention to, for the following reasons:

1) I intended to ask for an epidural very early, so breathing through any pain would be a wasted skill.
2) I knew that even if I paid attention in the class, when the actual event started I'd forget the minutes-between-contractions thing and simply go to the hospital once Ken and I thought of a middle name for the baby.
3) And finally, if I needed a C-section, any small amount of knowledge I'd picked up in class would not be needed by the doctors (at least I hoped it wouldn't).

When Holly finished torturing me with her ditty, I asked her, "How can you know so much? I run out of animals after three verses of 'Old McDonald.' "

She shrugged. "I just do," she said. I knew what she meant—it's how I feel when someone seems impressed (?) with my encyclopedic knowledge of the caloric content of almost any food. Some stuff is so fundamental you just absorb it.

Not so for calculus, children's songs—and how to draw a recognizable bunny rabbit. Lyric shortfall can extend beyond music to encompass arts-and-crafts. Stinking at one practically guarantees you'll need remedial help with the other. If you see a woman belting out "Peter Pointer's up and Peter Pointer's down/Peter Pointer's dancing all around the town," it's a good bet she's handy with glitter glue.

And unfortunately art, like singing, can be very public—like an orientation night for your son's preschool. At ours, the parents sat at tiny toddler tables, trying hard to think of something endearing to say as we went around the room introducing ourselves. Then the teacher handed out paper and crayons and suggested we draw a picture of something our child likes. "We'll hang it in his cubby so he'll feel welcome when he stows his lunch box."

I *wanted* to draw something for my boy, but I feared he'd run away crying about a "monster" in his cubby. I'd be called into the preschool director's office. "It's a horse," I'd be explaining, when the court-ordered psychiatrist analyzing my picture would conclude that my child should be placed in a home where the mother can draw a respectable Black Beauty.

Ken did manage to sketch a pretty good train at the orientation, but not every couple was lucky enough to include an artist. Looking down the table, I watched a perfectly dressed mother draw a shifty-looking Winnie the Pooh and then mutter to her husband, "Why should we have to draw—isn't that what we're paying them to do?"

But paying, I've found, is often what gets you into these exposed situations in the first place: you pay for a music-and-movement class and, next thing you know, you're required to do a two-step with your child in front of strangers. You pay to go to the zoo, and within hearing range of ten other families your kid's asking "What's that, Mommy?" "It's a, a, a," you say, stalling, as your eyes dart around the exhibit, frantically searching for the informational placard. "It's an onyx, of course, you silly billy."

But if there's any good news in song/art/zoo degradation, it's this: after a year or two of hanging out with a kid you *do* start to catch on, at least to the early childhood stuff. Although I still haven't learned the definition of a quark, I have learned to draw a rudimentary horse. In fact, if I'm feeling sad that my younger son never got the undivided attention his older brother enjoyed, I console myself with the thought that when it comes time for me to draw a picture to put in *his* preschool cubby, what I produce will definitely be recognizable as an animal—of some sort.

Chapter 8

Preschool for Scandal

∽⟳

$\mathcal{M}$ommy never thought she'd take her children to one of those indoor play spaces she'd seen other parents fall victim to. But then again, Mommy never thought she'd refer to herself as Mommy. Your idea of acceptable behavior changes once you have kids.

When my older son was about thirteen months old, and the preschool applications had me whipped into a panic over his slim résumé, I wrestled him and his supplies into the car and knowingly and willingly drove him to Gymboree. It was one of those glorious fall afternoons in New England, but instead of being outside enjoying the splendor of nature—for free—the two of us were sequestered inside a boxy room in a strip mall, sitting in a circle with little Ethan and Harry and Kaitlyn and Caitlin, singing along with Gymbo, the Gymboree clown (not an actual clown, but the leader's hand puppet). We were halfway into a song celebrating Thumbkin and Tall Man when I realized I'd been so focused on doing all the appropriate hand motions, and making eye contact with Gymbo, I hadn't even noticed that my son had left the circle and climbed atop a small slide with no side rails.

Not wanting to call attention to the fact that my child, and mine alone, had left the group, I was reluctant to rescue him from his perch, and yet a fall from the mini tower, followed by screaming, was likely to bring even greater disapproval from the crowd of *complete strangers*. I tried to remind myself that every other mommy was too focused on herself and her own child to worry about my little drama, and yet I couldn't help but feel I would be judged. Hmm. It was a close call, but in the end I put my son's safety first.

Approaching him slowly and respectfully—any sudden movement could alert him to my intentions and actually cause the very plunge I was trying to prevent—I spoke in the conciliatory tones used by law-enforcement officers coaxing hostage takers into releasing their captives unharmed. "Look at Gymbo! Isn't he silly! Mr. Thumbkin wants you to come and play."

But he held his ground. I flashed Gymbo the clown puppet one of those "kids do the darndest things" smiles (at least that's the look I was aiming for; I might have grimaced), and fished around in my knapsack for my cell phone so my son could bend its antenna, when Gymbo announced that song time was over and brought out a festive box. "Everyone take a music maker," Gymbo said. "A music maker!" I repeated. "Let's go!"

To my surprise, my son rejoined the group. A minute later I wished I had been more careful about what I wished for. Down among the crowd, he could cause extreme pain to innocent people—like me. Although I, too, sometimes want to rip something out of another's hands—like the last ripe avocado in the produce section—my fear of being recognized keeps me in check. But at Gymboree the challenge was to restrain someone for whom the sentence "People will talk" meant absolutely nothing.

To the naked eye, the maraca in Ethan's hand appeared identical to the twenty others in Gymbo's box, but to my son, possession of that maraca, and that maraca alone, was all that stood between him and total and complete happiness—for fifteen seconds at least. Like a skilled surgeon, he removed the maraca from Ethan's grasp. I tried to talk him out of it. I mentioned that he might want to return to the dangerous climbing structure—but he would have none of it. "Don't worry about it," Ethan's mother—the show-off—said sweetly, as her child quietly accepted a substitute. "Thank you," I said, looking at my watch. How much more of this child's play could I handle?

Mercifully, the class ended soon after the maraca episode and without further incident. On the trip home, for reasons that are unclear, I talked up the class as if I were selling my son a three-month membership. "Wasn't that fun!" I said. "Gymbo knows so many games." No answer from the back seat. I made a few more stabs at conversation—"You were wonderful under the colorful parachute!"—but after five minutes of putting all my mingling skills to work and still eliciting nothing, I felt I'd fulfilled my maternal duty. So I called Dana. (I know I'm not supposed to talk on my cell phone when I'm driving—but this was an emergency.) "I'm never going back to one of those classes," I told her. "Never." There was silence on the other end as she took in the news. Like many mothers, Dana had had her own mixed experience with children's classes. In her case, she was so busy playing up to a potential client during a Tumbling Tots gymnastics program that she lost track of her daughter completely. But even so, she was aghast at the idea that someone would be brave enough to renounce organized play, opting instead to sing and draw with her child—could it be possible?—on her own.

"You're not going to homeschool him, are you?" she asked.

Homeschool? A one-year-old? I confessed that I hadn't thought about it that way, but once I did, I knew that I was the last person who should be homeschooling anyone, particularly someone I loved. I thought back to my own school days. Every August I'd vow that the coming year would be different. I'd resolve to take legible notes—or at least take *some* notes, or, at the very least, *get* the notes from another student. But around mid-September I'd be back to my old tricks, and I feared any homeschooling efforts would meet with a similar fate. I'd start with the best intentions. My son and I would spend unstructured hours playing instruments we'd made from pots and pans, and making up fairy tales and finding found art. Each day would be an adventure in learning. But a week or two into the school year, my luck would change—I say "luck" because I have no control over my own behavior—and the teaching would basically end. We'd be driving over to a nature preserve or an animal refuge—I would have boasted widely about the activity—when I'd notice a FINAL REDUCTIONS sign in a store window, and I'd be overcome with a craving to shop, so I'd drive a little past our original destination and then—oops—my student would fall asleep in his car seat, virtually forcing me to check out the sale. "Just this once," I'd tell myself as I maneuvered the Graco into the big dressing room. "It's a Teacher Enrichment Day."

Or, we'd be listening to "Peter and the Wolf" at home, and I'd be dutifully saying "Let's listen for the clarinet's voice" when I'd realize it was the top of the hour and switch the CD player to NPR (wasn't it more important for my student to have a well-informed tutor?). I'd intend on returning to our music lesson, but then I'd hear a promo for an upcoming report on Tuscan olive growers from Sylvia Poggioli, or a Daniel Schorr commentary would start, and I'd completely forget my sacred role as an educator.

I'm not being modest when I say my son's education would be better off in Gymbo's hands or anyone else's. So even though we never returned to Gymboree, I started reading course catalogs for every organization within a fifteen-mile radius, and the semester my older son turned eighteen months old I had him enrolled in three courses, with his younger brother (age three and a half months) auditing. There was Music Together, Marcie and Me, and Movin' & Groovin'.

Not having been overly competitive in high school or college, I was surprised by my behavior in some of these classes, and by "surprised" I mean "disgusted." We'd be singing "Twinkle Twinkle" or doing pregymnastics, and I'd notice some other child properly holding his silvery star above his head and twisting it to the music, or tumbling as instructed, while my child would be playing by himself with a train he'd found in an off-limits part of the room.

Here's where the disgusting part comes in: I'd become just a little too eager to learn about the "Twinkle Twinkle" prodigy. Initiating small talk, I'd attempt to sound casual and then move in for the kill. "How old is he?" My own voice had the falsely blasé note I'd detected when other moms inquired about the age of *my* son after he aced a puzzle or named all the colors of a beach ball.

At first I wondered why I cared so much about who was 19 months and who was 19.25 months. Then I recognized my obsession as an obvious variation on the way I skim news stories about celebrated first-time novelists or Pulitzer Prize winners in search of the person's age. The relationship of that number to my own age determines whether I can read about his or her triumph without being thrust into despair.

After a while I stopped asking about the other kids, in part because I encountered a few mothers who actually lied about their kids' ages, shaving off a month or two, and in part because I stopped really caring. Or maybe there were just too many classes with too many students to measure ourselves against. Dance Your Tail Off, Yoga Adventure, Puddle Stompers, Creative Movement, Moving Together, Arts in the Park, Time for Partners, Gymsters. It was getting hard to keep track of the class times. In fact, I was starting to worry that I was using the classes as a crutch. That dark thought occurred to me—hit me in the face, actually—when I was walking my older son home from school and he lay down in the snow to make an angel. "Where'd you learn to do that?" I asked as he swished his arms and legs up and down. "In snow class," he said, unwittingly mocking me by mentioning a course too absurd to exist.

Or was it? When I got home I went on the Internet to see if I could find such an offering, because if there was one thing that drove me crazy—and there are obviously many—it was knowing there was a kiddie class out there that we weren't taking—Italian, organic cooking, poetry, cow milking, etiquette, violin, meditation. One day I was in an art class, trying to look Involved (while maintaining my distance from any paint, glue, crayons, glitter, or markers, lest a speck get on my favorite black T-shirt—which I shouldn't have worn, except I wanted to look good for the first class), when I overheard one mom asking another if her kids were going to do Crafty Critters or Community

Theater for Sprouts in the fall. *Crafty Critters? Community Theater for Sprouts?*

Should I admit I'd been eavesdropping? "Where?" I wanted to ask. "When? How old do the students have to be? Do they check birth certificates? Are there parental-participation requirements?"

That last question's crucial. You'll be discreetly whispering with another mother, or zoning out when you're supposed to be zooming and zipping, when the teacher will shoot you a look. As an adult, there's nothing more embarrassing than being reamed out by a teacher. They also dislike it if you don't seem interested enough in your child's output. This happened to me in the art class. In an attempt to prevent my younger son from covering himself completely in dark-purple paint (I didn't care about *his* clothing, but he's a big hugger), I picked up the piece of paper he'd soaked in paint and, holding it by a corner, an arm's distance away from my body, I headed toward the garbage can (hey, he'd already made two nice drawings we could save). Halfway to the trash barrel the teacher intercepted me. "Let's put that out in the hall so it can dry and you can take it home," she said, writing my son's name—first and last—in the only corner of the paper still exposed.

But even severe wardrobe threats pale in the face of a stress so palpable that it has permeated every class I've ever taken with my kids: the fear that your toddler will behave like—there's no nice way to say this—like a toddler.

You'll be in art or music or gym, and things will be going smoothly enough, when your child will remember that he's a kid and empty the glitter canister on the floor, or refuse to relinquish the trampoline, or run around the music room chasing another kid, instead of sitting in your lap and singing "Baa Baa Black Sheep." Or he'll stand by the door begging to leave, or demand a snack despite the NO FOOD signs posted around the room: that he can't read doesn't matter to the teacher.

The unimaginable—and yet all too imaginable—happened to one of the moms in a music class taught by a very talented—and very strict—young woman. One day her son, Simon, threw a tantrum when asked to return his little drum. *There but for the grace of God go I,* I thought. Simon's mom tensed as the instructor told her child to stop screaming and give back his instrument. "Immediately!"

The next week, the spot in the circle where Simon and his mom usually sat was empty. After class, during the brief period when the moms speed-socialize, one mother said she'd been in touch with the shamed one. "Apparently she got heart palpitations almost every class, and last week pushed her over the edge." We all assumed Simon and his mother were gone for good, but a few months later I heard they had signed up for another $190 semester.

At first I was surprised. But I gave it some thought and realized that of course the mother had no choice. After all, what was she going to do? Homeschool the kid?

Chapter 9

The Nap Artist

⟨૭⟩

*H*e was playing the innocence card. Staring at me with those big brown eyes, wrapping his soft little arms around my shoulders, breathing sweetly on my face—and it would have worked, too. If I hadn't been such a cold-blooded monomaniac, that is.

"Where are we going, Mommy?" my older son asked.

It was a fair question from someone who was being hustled, barefoot, into the back seat of a car along with his brother, when moments earlier he'd been happily playing with his trains. There'd been none of the familiar buildup that accompanies any trip. No ridiculously cheerful "Who wants to go to the grocery store for the paper towels I forgot to buy when we were there earlier?" No "Which big boys want to go to the dry cleaner's?"

I didn't want to lie—particularly since the awkward

moment a few months earlier when he'd caught me claiming a bag of M&M's was empty while in fact it was more than half full. But I feared that telling the truth—"I'm packing you boys into the car to induce simultaneous naps so I can read the new *New Yorker*"—would have a Cosa Nostra ring, even to a person who hadn't watched *The Sopranos*.

I felt like one of Tony's henchmen who'd been assigned to take care of a rat. "Hey Frankie, let's go for a drive."

"Why don't I have my shoes on?" my son asked. The kid was cute, but he had too many questions. "Don't worry," I whispered under my breath as I slipped *Sesame Street Platinum: All-Time Favorites* into the CD player. "Where you're going, you won't need shoes."

But that raised a big question: Where *was* he going once he was "sleeping with Elmo"? Back home again, where I'd gently lay him down in his bed? Or were he and his brother to remain in the car for the duration of their naps while I sat in the front seat quietly turning the pages of my magazine? This was not a decision to be made lightly. My top choice was to move the sleeping beauties inside so I could sit on the deck and enjoy "Talk of the Town" in the comfort of a chaise lounge, and pop up now and then to do laundry. (Pathetically, doing chores had entered the realm of fantasy.) But this option was very risky. If I carried the kids in from the car, the restfulness of one child or, more horribly, both, might not survive The Transfer. Then, instead of the two-hour break I needed to give me the strength and good cheer to make it through bath time, I'd be on Lego duty.

With the eternal "transfer/don't transfer" debate raging in my head, I headed my Honda slumber machine toward Route 9, where, if the traffic wasn't too heavy, I could get up some speed. And indeed, a few minutes later I was cruising toward the Land of Nod at forty miles per hour. The car was going forward, so I guess I should have been looking out the windshield, but I was more interested in what was happening in the back seat. My eyes were locked on the rearview mirror. Yes, it could be argued, this is a dangerous way to drive, but between the air bags and the car seats my kids and I could definitely survive an accident. A napless afternoon I wasn't so sure about.

A few miles later, the Back Seat finally closed its eyes—that's how Ken and I have come to think of the kids, as "the Back Seat." As in: the Back Seat wants juice. Or the Back Seat wants to hear "C is for Cookie," *not* "I Fall to Pieces." Looking for moral support before attempting the feared Double Transfer, I called Ken. He was working in the ER, and at the time of our conversation I think he was in the middle of saving a life, but we both knew who was under more pressure.

"I think you should go for it!" he said. "But don't rush it. Drive around for a while—take a cementing lap or two." I thanked the good doctor for his consultation. "But don't overshoot it," he added. "Don't miss your window. Stay in the sweet spot."

It was great advice, or would have been, except that neither of us knew how long the so-called cementing period should last or, just as important, how long we had before we overshot it. What we did know was this: if we transferred them out of the car too late in the sleep cycle they'd wake up, and what would have been a two-hour nap would be cruelly cut down to twenty minutes or less. And no second chances. Under their rules of engagement, a nap of any duration—even three minutes—meets the day's quota and knocks out all subsequent naps. If one of my sons closes his eyes in the car on the way to Trader Joe's—four-tenths of a mile away—that will be it until tomorrow.

I performed one of those mental exercises where you picture yourself successfully completing the task at hand. But instead of giving me confidence, it spooked me. As I imagined myself easing one boy after the other into his respective sleeping quarters, my stomach tightened and my mind's ear heard toddler screams. My stress level was that of someone about to defuse a bomb, not of a mother poised to move two sweet little children from a sedan into a condo.

I decided to settle for the car-based nap. I pulled back into the parking spot in front of our building, made sure the boys were still breathing, and raced inside to microwave a few soy nuggets. On the way out of the apartment with my hot lunch, I grabbed the cordless phone, and then I settled into my home-next-to-home. If only I could have installed a StairMaster and a dorm fridge I'd have been all set.

After dining, I called my dad to say a very quiet hello. "It's too bad you can't get the car into the apartment," he said. The ultimate can-do person, he was trying to figure a way to drive the vehicle into our living room, when my call-waiting clicked.

It was Allison, the only person I know who's almost been arrested for a nap-related offense. She was calling from the front seat of her SUV.

Her son absolutely will not survive the Transfer and won't fall asleep at home, so Allison spends two hours a day, and sometimes three, in her car. You can read or even do limited grocery shopping at the drive-through Dunkin' Donuts (milk, bagels) and McDonald's (salad, ketchup), but after a while confinement, even in a luxury vehicle, does things to a person.

In the beginning, Allison's behavior, while admittedly extreme, had not forced her to go underground. She'd drive to a store where she had a DVD to return, or ice cream to buy, and she'd idle out front until a friendly-looking person walked by, at which point she'd call out from her window and ask the pedestrian if he'd mind popping into the Blockbuster or 7-Eleven.

People were almost always willing to help, but even so, she tired of relying on the kindness of strangers. She began allowing herself to leave the car and take short walks, keeping her snoozing son in view. This proved to be a gateway activity. Allison began allowing herself to enter a store (without enlisting a watchman) as long as she could see her car from the shop. One day she parked outside a children's shop on a busy street, rolled down the car windows a crack, locked the vehicle, and darted into the boutique. She was working the sale racks when she overheard another customer reporting that a sleeping child was alone in a car outside the store. Hoping to allay the meddling (and continue shopping), Allison piped up. "He's mine—I can see him from here."

She should have fled immediately, she told me later, but after acknowledging it was her child, she was drawn to a sign announcing a major markdown on shoes at the rear of the store. She was considering a pair of kiddie Nikes when the owner confronted her. "The police are on their way."

Allison dropped the Nikes and bolted. Her heart pounding, her foot heavy on the gas, she blew through yellow lights and left the main road as fast as possible. Screeching onto a side street and down a long driveway with good foliage cover, she turned off her engine and waited out the cops (all without waking her son, she told me proudly—the criminal's boast). But the shoes—"That killed me, they were down to ten dollars."

I assumed her brush with the law would have scared her straight, but she was too far gone to stop. "I can't let myself just sit in the car for hours on end," she said.

"But you *could*," I pointed out, "cut his naps to an hour. You'd have less time behind the wheel." This piece of advice was in the "Do as I say, not as I do" category, since everyone

I knew (except for Allison) was advising me to shorten my own kids' naps to one hour, in hopes they would sleep later in the morning, or through the night. Their choice.

"I never let Sarah go more than fifty minutes, an hour tops," Dana told me. "Absolutely start waking them up."

It sounded harsh, but I knew she was trying to be nice, in a "Friends don't let the children of friends nap so long" way.

I started to protest—"But I need the time to get stuff done"—but Dana told me to do the nap math: except on the weekends, the kids are snoozing on someone else's watch.

"Your nanny is getting the hours that belong to you," she said.

I ran the numbers, and sure enough, Dana was right. I was ready to ban naps altogether, until I remembered a sad truism: There are no guarantees in life, which is guaranteed when it comes to children's sleep habits. An infant who sleeps through the night from the ages of three months to six months will suddenly turn on his parents, and start waking every hour. Or a child known far and wide for singing herself to sleep in the crib will suddenly require a ninety-minute parental serenade before she's willing to go down.

Knowing my kids, I'd shorten their naps and then, in the same unfair way your metabolism slows if you go on a very low calorie diet, the boys would learn to manage with less sleep. I can just hear my older son laying out the battle plan to his accomplice: *If she starts waking us after an hour, I'll go back to my five-fifteen rooster's call, and you revert to crying at three A.M.*

The more I thought about it, the more I realized that even if the kids were to start sleeping later or more soundly, *I* wasn't ready to make the transition. I needed "my" two-hour nap. I'd come to depend on it. Technically, of course, I wasn't the one sleeping, but as any parent knows, the nap is not the child's, but rather it belongs to the person on duty at the time of the slumber (as in, "Did he nap for you?").

Besides, there's something special about nap time. I think Allison put her finger on it. "During nap time, you get credit for spending time with your kids even if you're doing your nails." Since you're not paying a baby-sitter, there's no pressure to be productive. It's like having a merchandise credit. Yes, the money—or in this case the hours—was yours in the first place, but still it feels like you're getting something for free.

But unlike a merchandise credit, the nap is filled with uncertainty: When will it happen? How long will it last? What if it's too late and leads to wakefulness at bedtime?

But like the old joke, *the food's terrible and the portions are too small*, even as I complain about nap-related tension, I'm dreading the day when my sons give up their naps. I used to believe this would happen in the same way a marriage breaks down—slowly, and with warning signs. But I know that's not true, either. You can be chopping cilantro in your newly renovated kitchen, thinking all is well, only to have your spouse return one evening and announce he's Met Someone. A reliable napper can quit cold turkey, too.

I came upon this little tidbit—only the single most important piece of child care information in existence—almost by accident, in *What to Expect: The Toddler Years*. Much to my surprise, the authors treat the threat very casually. "Sometimes a toddler gives up his nap prematurely because of a one-time event that knocked his schedule out of whack," they write. "An afternoon birthday party or trip to the movies, a weekend at Grandma's (where it's too fun to sleep)."

Here's what I don't understand: the Consumer Product Safety Commission saturates the media with recalls of products harmful to the public, and a notice wasn't sent out about this? Where are people's priorities? With a shudder, I shut *What to Expect*. My kids would never again go to a birthday party, movie, or Grandma's.

As it would happen, a few days later I got a call from "Grandma," up to her nap-killing tricks, telling me about a wonderful vacation house she'd rented on an island off the coast of Maine.

It sounded like the perfect place for a family trip—to the untrained ear: a heated pool, beaches, a few playgrounds. "And no cars allowed," my mother added. To her, that was a selling point; to me, a giant red flag. Without the benefit of an engine,* I couldn't be sure of nap inducement. This benign family weekend, in other words, could be the very one-time no-doze event the *What to Expect* writers warned against.

"We can't go," Ken said, only half joking.

But in the end we decided to risk it—our stroller's 85 percent effective in the napping department. When we arrived on the island, a better option immediately presented itself: the van—the only vehicle allowed—that drove guests from the ferry to their rental cottages. I looked at Ken. "Are you thinking what I'm thinking?"

"See if he can pick us up tomorrow at noon," Ken whispered. If that wasn't permitted, we'd pretend we were leaving the island a day ahead of schedule, and needed a ride to the boat, and then . . . change our minds, say we'd forgotten something back in the cottage, and by then the kids would be asleep.

Luckily, we didn't need to resort to subterfuge, and even luckier, the island getaway didn't snuff out the naps. But a

---

* If there's one problem with using your car as a nap machine, it's—actually there are three problems: 1) You're in a very vulnerable position if your car's in the shop; 2) You can't take an island vacation; and 3) Your child may start to build up a tolerance. I can barely admit this to myself, but I think—no, I know—it's happening to my older son. Where the simple act of strapping him into his car seat used to be soporific, now we have to hit highway speeds. One night Ken drove him fifty miles without effect. "I'm sorry," Ken said as the two of them walked side by side through the front door—mission *not* accomplished—"but I had to come home. I was falling asleep behind the wheel."

second family vacation, to Montreal with Ken's side of the equation, almost did us in. Ken's parents had very nicely agreed to take on morning baby-sitting duties, and without going into the boring details, I'll just say it was crucial to our plans that neither child had napped when we retook custody at 11 A.M.

On the second day of the trip, Ken went up to his parents' hotel room half an hour before the designated pickup time (to get a guidebook, not to conduct a spot-check), and he came upon a scene that was heartbreaking in its sweetness—and straight out of our own personal horror flick: his mother had our younger boy tucked into bed, and was not only singing to him, but was massaging his head. Luckily, Ken had burst in just in time to stop the lullaby and keep our child awake until it was our turn to watch him (sleep).

"I'm still scared thinking about how close it was," I told Ken an hour later, as we packed the kids into the car and went for a little . . . drive.

Chapter 10

Meet the Grandparents

$\mathcal{W}$here have all the grandparents gone?

I don't mean literally. We know exactly where they *are*: they're at Pilates, or getting a Botox fix. Maybe Gramps is with his personal trainer, or taking in an indie film at Sundance. And Granny? She's not bent over a stove in a housecoat, or knitting in the parlor, that's for sure. She's in her home office, updating her Web site, or in Washington, D.C., leading a protest march against cuts in education funding.

The modern breed's so different that even their homes are unrecognizable. Where's the smell of kasha? The table pads that must be put on the dining room table even for snacktime? What happened to the plastic slipcovers? The Old World accents?

But the problem goes beyond cosmetics. It's not just that

this generation doesn't look, sound, or smell like grandparents—there's an entire subset that doesn't act like them either. Not all, of course, or even most. But there are some—and believe me, you'll know immediately—who are not quite, how shall I say, trustworthy in the child care department.

Not that they're begging to watch your child anyway. Dana's parents have such full schedules that the last thing they want to do is hang around the house with some kid or, worse yet, endure a trip to the zoo or the aquarium. "Their way of being grandparental is to pay for a baby-sitter," she told me.

Things have gotten so convoluted that where once new moms used to swap "You won't believe what he did" tales about clueless husbands, now the dads are right there with their spouses, piously aghast at some child care atrocity committed by their parents or in-laws. "Grandma put the baby to sleep on his belly instead of his back!" "Well, ours forgot to turn on the baby monitor." This is the new way couples bond.

I'm waiting for Hollywood's *next* sequel to *Three Men and a Baby*. The last one, as you may recall, was *Three Men and a Little Lady*, in which Tom Selleck, Steve Guttenberg, and Ted Danson played bachelors raising a five-year-old girl. But that was 1990, a time when fathers—not grandparents—were unreliable. Today's blockbuster would be *Five Grandparents and a Baby*, and audiences would roar with laughter and (quiet) recognition as Alan Alda and his second wife, Diane Keaton, and his ex, Goldie Hawn, and her second ex, Albert Brooks, and her new lover, Harrison Ford, baby-sit Alda's and Hawn's son's infant for forty-eight hours while the baby's parents go off on a romantic weekend, unaware of the perils menacing their child.

If the great outdoors is involved, there's even more reason to worry when grandparents are "watching" the kids. I called Allison one afternoon when her parents had taken her son to the beach, and she was so distracted she could barely hold a conversation. "Do you think I should drive over and try to find them?"

"What happened to all the *real* grandparents?" I said, by way of response. But she was no longer on the phone. I called—who better?—my own mother. Fresh from a morning of kayaking, she was about to lift weights before going off to an Arts Council meeting. My question prompted her to recall a summer when we'd rented a house in Connecticut. "I think you were three years old," she began. "You'd go out in the morning and play on the street with a little boy who lived in the neighborhood. You'd come back in for lunch and then you'd go out again."

"I was outside *alone*? What were you doing at the time?"

MOM: "I don't know—hanging out in the house, I guess. Reading, probably."

ME: "I was three? And I entertained myself all day?

You weren't worried I'd get hit by a car or something?"

MOM: "You might have been four."

Today, of course, you could never let your preschooler
play unsupervised in your own neighborhood. Even if she
wasn't snatched up or injured, you'd have to move—because
of the gossip. But things were different back then. Or at
least that's what grandparents always claim. They'll tell you
the most incredible story—that when you were six you
made delicious steaks on an open-pit barbeque, or that at
eighteen months you loved sleeping on the top bunk, or that
for your third birthday you had a lawn darts party. And
when you express surprise at being allowed to engage in
these dangerous activities, they'll say, "Well, things were
different back then."

And there's no way to check. There were no Mommy
Cams at the time. And, to be fair, raising kids wasn't always
such a production. As Allison told her mother, "Mom, you
don't know what it's like to be a mother." Crazy? Well, yes
and no. Now we know that a cuddly teddy bear can be used
as a handy ladder by an enterprising child bent on scaling
the crib's railing. Peanut butter, once *the* snack of the preschool set, has been outlawed from many areas as Public Al-
lergen Number One. (Anthrax causes less alarm than a jar
of Skippy.) And beach balls? Ours is imprinted with a long
list of warnings, including "Never leave in or near water

when not in use," and concludes with this cheerful thought: "Follow these rules to avoid drowning, paralysis, or other serious injury." Let the fun begin! And that's just a beach ball. Think what the beach could do.

I was reading a parenting magazine when I came upon a survey: "Who's a Better Mom? You or Your Mother?" I thought that was pretty mean-spirited—why pit the generations against each other?—but even so, I took the test. I thought about how kind and loving my mother is, and how she used to tell me that if people weren't nice to me it was because they were "jealous," and how she used to edit my articles before I filed them with my actual editors, and still recalls the names of my high school friends' boyfriends. I love her joyful outlook on life, and I could go on, but I think you can guess who was going to get my vote. But even as I was checking off the box with her name, I wondered how she'd fare in today's hypercautious world. Sure, she's a stickler about cleanliness and nutrition, but her position on car seats?

"I believe in them when they're convenient," she told me.

The subject arose a few weeks ago. I was taking the kids to a birthday party, and since Ken needed the car for work I'd called a cab. I was on the phone with my mom when the driver rang our bell. "Wish me luck," I said, "I've got to install the car seats while keeping the kids at bay." Even as the words left my mouth, I knew I'd revealed too much. "Beth, if you lived in New York, you'd be taking cabs without car seats all the time," she said. "You're right," I said, "I'll yell 'Pretend we're in Manhattan' if we're about to crash."

Her case-by-case-basis position on car seats is in keeping with her favorite story. One day when I was a toddler, my mother and I were driving in my parents' convertible. The top was down and I was not buckled in. My mom had just pulled off the FDR Drive onto 96th Street when the guy next to her started to honk his car's horn. "Lady," he called out, "your baby is crawling out the back of your car." The thing about this story that gets me is that it's never told with a shudder, or in a "What if?" way, recognizing that we'd luckily avoided a tragedy, but rather in an "Oh, well, what will be will be" tone. "Things were different back then," my mother said.

The grandparents aren't *trying* to be negligent. They don't need to be put in a time-out, or to be told "Buckle that grandchild into his high chair before I count to three, or Mommy's going to be very angry." It's simply that a lot of our precautions are as beyond their familiar routines as blogging.

Holly's father was watching her children for a few hours, and when she returned home, much to her surprise, they were both napping. "Really dead to the world," she told me. "How'd you do it?" she asked her father. "Marsala always works," he replied. She was confused. "They were crying," he explained, "so I put it on their gums and they fell right asleep." So much for abstaining while she breast-fed.

Holly was in her late thirties when she had her second baby, which meant that the grandparents were no spring chickens, either. "I was so focused on my biological clock that I forgot to think about *theirs*," she said. Her husband's parents are "starting to forget things," she told me, like the fact that their neighbor parks his car in the same spot on the street every day. More than once, her father-in-law has pulled out of his driveway and smashed into it. "What's *that* doing there?" he asks. Ever the sweetie, Holly started lying to avoid having Grandpa drive her children around. "I say they suffer from motion sickness."

Not everyone is so diplomatic, however. "The word 'trust' is tricky," Allison said. "I can *trust* my parents with my son in the sense that I know they won't invite a cute boy over and raid the liquor cabinet or watch MTV the whole time they're supposed to be watching him, but it's not total peace of mind. My parents love to comment on the fact that I'm 'such a first-time mom,' and involving them means that I will have to hear this or get defensive. 'You're right, Mom, I don't particularly *want* my child to get all of his fiber by chewing windowsills.'

"And forget trying to get them to discipline," she continued. "They've been through all of that once before and are now just in it for the fun. This is not speculation—my dad had told me as much."

The new moms and dads aren't the only ones dying to gossip. I can't tell you how many grandparents I've talked to who couldn't wait to share with me—a stranger—stories about their own children and their child-rearing habits. I met a grandmother in line at the grocery store who saw my boys as an entrée into conversation. "I have a new grand-daughter . . . they're calling her Madison Ashley," she said, with obvious distaste.

"What a beautiful name," I replied, too busy fending off candy requests to get into criticizing someone I've never met (usually I'm more than willing to do this).

"Well," she said tartly, "it wouldn't have been *my* choice."

And there's another thing different about today's grand-parents. Their names. In the days of yore, Grandma and Grandpa were, well, "Grandma" and "Grandpa." But now they're too young for that, so they must be called by their first names, or something French or Japanese or some other ethnicity they only know from a restaurant. I read about a boomer who has her grandchildren call her Moogie, the term for mother in *Star Trek: Deep Space Nine*, and about others called Minnow and FaFa. It won't be long before publishers start putting out books of potential grandparent names. You'll see expectant grandparents standing in the bookstore, leafing through *The Greatest Granny Names Ever* or *Beyond Bubbe and Zaide*. "Duke: an old English name, meaning he who will not change diapers," or "Zsa-Zsa: from Hollywood, meaning she who only buys little girls fussy, impractical outfits and teaches boys to mix martinis." And that won't be the last of it. There will be Web sites where grandparents can find out what celebrity grandparents are called.

As nice a gesture as it seems, if you let your parents choose their own grand-names, you either have to live with the results or try to nix what they come up with—risking a family feud with the very people whose help you're going to need over the next few years. Allison found herself in a sensitive veto situation. Not long before her child was born, her father announced he wanted to be called "Papa." "Paaaa-paaa," Allison called out, as if she were an Italian child in an arty Italian film. "Why don't we just go all the way and call you Gepetto?" she asked.

But it's hard for the grandparents to hit it just right. For every adult child complaining that his or her parents refuse to act the part of grandparents, there's an adult child complaining that his or her parents are *too* into their new roles, entirely forgetting the middlemen. One of my colleagues at the *Herald* is in that situation. One day I saw a group of new moms gathered around as she held court. "You know how they talk about things skipping a generation?" she asked rhetorically. "I'm the generation that's being skipped. My mother is obsessed with my daughter. She won't let her walk from the living room to the kitchen because she might trip on the carpet. When I was little, I was allergic to onions, but my mother never took it seriously. So now it turns out that my daughter is lactose intolerant, and my mother has essentially wiped dairy out of her own diet. She drinks only soy now. She keeps no butter in her refrigerator. She uses different utensils—it's as if she's keeping kosher."

Each member of the group was waiting to tell her own grandparental story, and although I had to leave to do some work, when I returned sometime later, the griping was still in full swing.

Yet, for all the complaining, I can't say I've noticed anyone passing up the free baby-sitting.

Chapter 11

If Nanny Ain't Happy, Ain't Nobody Happy

Whose happiness is more important—my nanny's or my children's?

I wish I could say, "What kind of mother would even ask that question?" But when you spend more time stocking the fridge for the sitter than for your sons, it's time to take a good hard look at yourself.

It's not that I don't care about my boys. It's that I care so much that I want the best child care possible, and if that means making sure my beloved nanny* has her favorite soy

---

* Like "fiancé," the word "nanny" sounds annoyingly high-end and embarrasses you at first. When Ken and I got engaged, "fiancé," with its accent, backed me into saying things like "My boyfriend and I are getting married in November." When I returned to work after my first maternity leave, I'd say, "Thankfully, we have a terrific *baby-sitter* who comes

protein drink from a health food store so inconvenient I can't go to the normal supermarket for the kids' supplies, so be it. Deep down, I know I'm doing it for my babies.

You know the old saying: If nanny ain't happy, ain't nobody happy. Especially not Mama.

The other day, as I was vacuuming before our nanny, Paula, arrived—I don't want OSHA sniffing around—I recalled those stories I'd heard when I was pregnant about how children put a damper on romance. I'd assumed fatigue and endless diaper conversations—"Do you smell something?" "I don't know, do you?"—chilled the lust. But the kids are only indirectly responsible. The truth is, it's *you* who are at fault. When you spend all your energy courting Mary Poppins, buying her little just-because-you're-great gifts, scouring Hallmark stores for cute cards, renewing your cable TV package so she can watch E!, subscribing to things you'd never read so she'll have something standing by when your two little darlings are—ahem—napping, there's no time to think about Daddy . . . what's his name again?

Or anyone else. Friends, coworkers, family members. Mom, I'm sorry I didn't bring you anything from London, but I was too busy. No, not sightseeing . . . Although I'd spent months planning the trip, preparing lists of theater

---

to the house while I work," i.e., a nanny. But now nannies have become cappuccinoed, which is to say anyone can have one, even someone like me, who doesn't have a decent set of cloth placemats and coordinating napkins. So how, you ask, can one sound fancy these days? Skip right over the tempting "au pair" and tell people you have a governess.

productions and art exhibits, once there I had no time to do anything but shop for our nanny. That gift was a minefield. It had to say, "You're the single most important person in our lives," and yet it couldn't be so nice it would give off a desperate vibe. Sort of like buying a present for a guy you've dated once (but have already decided you're going to marry) when his birthday happens to fall two days into your "relationship."

"Should I FedEx her a postcard?" I asked Ken when we touched down at Heathrow. The gift search took so much out of me that when we returned I really needed a vacation. If we could only get away—*away* away, this time. But that would necessitate another gift, restarting the whole stressful cycle.

So what did I buy her? A scarf from Harrods. That was four days into the trip (then I thought better and returned it). On the eighth day, I bought her a gift pack of chocolate double-decker buses. I had eaten them by the tenth day, which made me so anxious I could barely sleep, and then, on Day 11, I found It: a Big Ben–shaped tin filled with her favorite orange tea. We still had two days left. I hadn't seen the British Museum or *Much Ado About Nothing* but that didn't matter. I'd gotten what I'd come for.

When I reenter my world after a long trip—a weekend or a day away—after weighing myself, I head to the phone to be debriefed by My People (as Ken calls my friends). I was on my third such call, mid–Harrods scarf, when Holly gasped. "I have to call you back," she said.

What? Had Harrods, or my eating the chocolates, disgusted her? No, in that case she wouldn't have promised to call back. Perhaps one of her children had been injured? No, she'd have asked me what to do. Because Ken is a pediatrician, friends come to me for medical advice when they don't want to bother him. ("I'm an honorary nurse practitioner," I explained to Ken when he was surprised to overhear me diagnosing strep throat over the phone one morning.) Could Holly have seen a burglar—or had she noticed that the sage green in her couch clashed with—and not accented—the throw cushions?

No. It was worse. The Harrods scarf had jogged her memory. The day before had been her nanny's birthday, and she'd forgotten. Like writing a vicious e-mail and mistakenly addressing it to the subject and hitting "Send," or accidentally drinking a regular Coke instead of a Diet Coke (an outrage that actually happened to me, but that's a whole other book), Holly's lapse seemed beyond damage control.

What to do? Fake temporary amnesia? (It works on soap operas frequently.) Double the nanny's salary? (Expensive, but worth considering.)

While I was trying to comfort Holly, I realized that there's a profound gap in all the "fear of abandonment" literature. It focuses on the child's fear of losing his or her parents, which of course would be tragic, but how likely is that really? Between cell phone records and ATM withdrawals, the kids would have no trouble tracking you down. Why has nothing been written about the more likely scenario, in which the mother is abandoned by the nanny?

Unfortunately, I'm speaking from experience.

When my older son was about a year old, and our next guy was due in two months, my first nanny—the orange-tea recipient—uttered the dreaded words: "We have to talk." She explained, or tried to (I had covered my ears with my hands and was humming loudly), that increased family obligations (hers, not mine) meant she'd have to leave us.* I handled the news like the mature woman motherhood had made me. I threatened to kidnap her relatives. I offered her my first- and second-born children (which would have solved the problem quite neatly). I pretended to call a trial lawyer. But she was resolute. (Maybe I should have given her the scarf after all.)

Eventually, I looked on the bright side—which was the only side left—and did that thing where you tell all of your friends, "I'm glad he broke up with me, he was too perfect and I think that would have bugged me down the line." In the nanny version of this self-pep talk, I had the comforting thought that I'd no longer have to face the witness to my most humiliating new-mother moments. She's the one who knows that, five weeks into motherhood, I had

---

* As despondent as I was about losing her—and for months afterward I could barely look at the honey-filled bear she used to use for her tea—I was also worried about my reputation. Lose too many nannies, and people start to think it's *you*. This was strike one. My first divorce.

From Here to Maternity

no idea how my own baby liked to be held—or, for that matter, that there were different holds available. She heard the screams that accompanied diaper changes under my watch. She was there when I returned from work, all smiles, only to receive the most blasé greeting you can imagine from an eight-month-old. (There were times when I considered hiding a toy in my hand and flashing it at him when I got home, just so he'd throw a smile my way in her presence, or setting off the fire alarm in hopes his frown would get lost in all the confusion.)

I'm not sure why I cared so much. Anyone observing my eagerness would have assumed that I was auditioning to be the nanny for *her* children. On Mondays I'd make sure to tell her about cute little outings we'd taken over the weekend, almost as if I was trying to prove that I was good with kids. On Fridays I'd mention child-friendly activities we had planned, and I never, never let on that Ken's parents would be watching our boy come Sunday afternoon. Who knows what motivated me? Perhaps I feared she'd set up a Mommy Cam to snag me talking on the phone when I was supposed to be playing with finger puppets, or skipping ahead as we read *The Cat in the Hat*. I'd be shown in grainy footage at trial, condensing the lovely Dr. Seuss story to three pages, and the prosecutor, in his summation, would point at me and thunder to the jury, "She cheated on Thing One."

I was so busy reliving old, painful moments that the ringing of the phone startled me. "I called the florist and he solved the problem." It was Holly, of forgotten-nanny-birthday fame. She sounded as relieved as someone who's just gotten good medical news. "He's going to pretend that *he* messed up the delivery date.

"I feel sort of creepy," she added. "But I have no choice. This is my life we're talking about."

Holly spent $60 on the bouquet, which I thought was very generous. So generous that it unnerved me. Maybe I wasn't doing enough for my nanny. What if she decided to upgrade employers? Maybe to someone who doesn't even have kids? I decided that when Paula arrived the next day I'd have the kids bathed, changed, played with, read to, and fed. They could spend all day watching TV with her. Or maybe I'd hand her the car keys and give her the day off. "Get your nails done, work out, meet friends for lunch," I'd say. "You need some time to yourself."

That should do it, I thought. I was also willing to quit my job and stay home with the boys full-time, so she could enjoy herself during the day. She's so wonderful I'd hate to lose her.

Especially after what we went through to hire her. Paula had been the live-in nanny for a colleague of Ken's, and came highly recommended. We were so eager to impress her that we "joked" about hiring a child actor to play our son during the interview. Before the meeting we put out fresh flowers, lit a candle in the bathroom, and baked bread, not unlike Realtors preparing for an open house. We then turned our attention to our son, who had developed a runny nose just prior to her arrival. But wiping it was likely to set off a firestorm that would be in full swing when she arrived, and audible through the front door. Opting for the lesser of two evils, we left the nose pretty much as was, except for a kiss/wipe, and then the doorbell rang.

As Ricardo Montalban said on *Fantasy Island*, "Smiles, everyone, smiles."

Sweet, articulate, upbeat, conversant in dinosaurs and construction vehicles, Paula was everything we could have hoped for. A second date was arranged. Unfortunately the runny nose progressed to a cold and we feared he might not be . . . himself. "We've got to get him off-site," Ken said. Yes, I know that *the* most important factor in deciding whether to hire a person to care for your child is how she is with that child, but *her* we didn't have any doubts about. Why let our boy blow a wonderful opportunity for himself?

He was whisked off to Ken's parents' house. When Paula arrived and peered around corners looking for him, we glanced at our watches as if we, too, were surprised he wasn't home. "He's with his grandparents," I explained. "We were hoping he'd be home by now, but they can never bear to part with him."

I know what you may be thinking. I know what *I'd* be thinking if someone else told me this story. I also know what all of my friends and relatives said when I told it to them: "Are you crazy? You're paying good money to have someone care for your children, and you're worried about pleasing *her*?"*

I agree, but it's a competitive world out there. Everyone knows how hard it is to get into nursery school, but landing an Ivy League–quality nanny is just as difficult, particularly when the job you're offering is caring for a newborn *and* a fourteen-month-old. When we were in the process of looking, I'd see flyers around town—"Nanny sought for adorable four-year-old"—that made me sick with anxiety. "Enjoy our pool and summer house and fresh veggies from our garden. Access to a car. Opportunities for international travel."

Here's what my flyer would have said: "Rugs vacuumed every two weeks!"

"Wish me luck," I told Ken one night as I headed out to rip down the "adorable four-year-old" signs. "Those parents are trying to steal our nanny." I could already imagine the APB that would crackle over police radios. "We're looking for a crazed pregnant woman. She's considered hungry and extremely dangerous."

I don't know if Paula missed the flyer about the free car

---

* Nannies aren't the only people who sometimes need to be kept in the dark. Allison, like many women I know, has become very "vague" with her husband (and certain nosy relatives) about how much child care she gets each week.

"I keep needing more and more hours of help," she confessed one day. Like others involved in illicit behavior, she goes to great lengths to hide the Nanny Creep. She rearranges her schedule to make sure she's the one home to pay the woman, and if she absolutely can't be there, she puts the money in an envelope. "Sealed."

From Here to Maternity

and organic vegetables, or if the aroma of our freshly baked bread did its job, but she actually came to work for us right before our second son was born. At that point I was ready to sit back and relax, happy that my child care needs were being met, until one night a few months later when Ken and I wanted to do something really wild—see a movie on a screen bigger than our twenty-inch TV—and I realized that we didn't know any nighttime baby-sitters.

Time to start looking, but where? The relationship gurus say the best place to meet Someone is at an activity you both enjoy. Such as . . . a kiddie gymnastics class.

Yes, I should have been focusing on my older son's tumbling feats that morning at the YMCA. But really, I couldn't take my eyes off the teacher: peppy, wholesome, creative. "Mommy, look at me," my son—I think—yelled from the mini-tramp. I'd been daydreaming about the instructor. "You're great!" I called out to my boy, giving him a thumbs-up.

I decided to go for it with the instructor. "Do you, uh . . . What are you doing after work?" She knew what I was after, despite my clumsiness. "Sorry," she said, "but we're not allowed to accept baby-sitting jobs from people we meet here."

Motherhood had turned me into a pickup artist, always on the prowl for sweet young things to watch my sweet young things. The supermarket cashier who chuckled when my kids disabled the credit card machine? Can she do Friday nights? The waitress who brought extra crayons and straws, stat? I'll give her the biggest tip she's ever seen. And then there was the coed I stopped on the street. Her college sweatshirt carried the name of a school *known* for its early-education program. What a turn-on!

In retrospect, I realize that the gymnastic teacher's "no" meant "no," but at the time I thought she was like one of those sources I encounter as a journalist—eager to talk, but afraid someone's watching. "Stamp your foot twice if you're interested," I whispered as we locked eyes over the balance beam. "My number's in the book."

Like a schoolgirl with a crush, I sat by the phone, but gymnastics rolled around again with no word. In class, co-spotting my kid on the uneven bars, neither of us mentioned last week's come-on.

Driving home, I was wondering what I'd done wrong—was I not enthusiastic enough about my son's back somersault?—when my car was rear-ended at a red light. Jolted out of my shame spiral, I jumped out of the vehicle to talk to the other driver. It was a young woman. "I'm so sorry," she said. "I don't know what happened—I wasn't even on my cell phone." She wrote down her license and registration, but I wanted a different number: her cell. She looked like baby-sitting material. "She seems really nice," I told Ken later. "She doesn't have to chauffeur the kids around."

But this time I was the one who didn't call. We ended up inheriting a baby-sitter from a neighbor who moved. I was thrilled—and panicked that she'd call when Paula was home. What if she found out I was seeing another woman on the side? Especially on Saturday nights.

Mommy Dating: The Rules

⟨◌⟩

My older son didn't realize it, but this was our debut, if not into Society, at least into the world of finished basements and backyard swing sets. We were on our first formal playdate ever, with one of the coolest mom-child pairs in his preschool class. (Flirting at morning drop-offs and parent breakfasts had paid off.) And the best part? There was real chemistry happening with the four of us around the little Pottery Barn Kids table.

In fact, after The Other Woman served cookies without inquiring about wheat, lactose, peanut, or soy allergies, or pretending her child usually only ate fruit, I'd started to get that heady "this could really work out" feeling, the kind you experience for the first time when you meet the guy you want to marry and he feels the same way about you, and then the second time when you and your (now) husband get asked out on a double date by another couple that you have a couples crush on.

The Other Woman and I were doing that end-of-the-date dance, where you say "We should do this again," and to show that it's not just the old "I'll call you" line, you each pull out a Palm Pilot (or in my case a scrap of paper from the bottom of my knapsack) to set a date. In other words, everything was going perfectly—I'd managed to coat and boot my child with a minimum of resistance—when my smaller half grabbed one of his host's trucks and hugged it to his new corduroy overalls (yes, bought just for the date). "It's mine," he yelled. It was such a textbook display of two-berty* that I felt as if I were watching a child actor on TV.

When you're on a double date in the adult world, if your partner behaves poorly it doesn't reflect on you. The other couple may wonder why you're with a cad, but they don't hold you responsible. But when you're dating with your child, not only is his behavior a direct reflection on you—in an unspoken, "she seems nice, but there must be something going on at home" way—but how you deal with the situation counts, too.

In fairness, I should say that I've fallen victim to this

---

* When it comes to wild mood swings, emotional outbursts, and the fight for independence from the parents, puberty gets all the attention. But anyone who lives with a child transitioning from the Infant section of Baby Gap to Toddler, from Teletubbies to Dora the Explorer, knows that the two-bescent child is every bit as hormonal as his fourteen-year-old cousin.

same kind of last-minute temptation as my son, only in my case it's usually a good thing—even when I complain, "I was almost safely out of J. Crew when I spotted a [fill in the blank], which set off an entire round of buying." At some level I'm happy to have made the purchases, or I wouldn't have gone shopping in the first place.

Mixed emotions played no part in the current situation.

For starters, I wanted to get home so we could begin the "I don't want to get into the bath" and the subsequent "I don't want to get out of the bath" fights on time. I also knew The Other Woman had people coming over that night and needed to get started in the kitchen, something her good manners prevented her from doing while a brawl was under way in the basement.

As I tried to loosen my partner's grip on the vehicle, I thought about something Dana had said when I told her I was having a boy. "When he gets to be about two he'll be like your little boyfriend."

I recalled how I'd imagined me and my two-year-old significant other lingering over dinners and arguing (in a loving way) about independent films and politics, and I pictured him buying me little gifts. "This reminded me of you," he'd say in a foreign accent. (I wasn't sure why he'd have an accent—Ken and I are native English speakers—but it was a fantasy, so why quibble?) And then, after we'd become like one, we soul mates would venture out into the world on our first double date.

Sometimes when one child is laying claim to another

child's toy, the owner's mother will whisper, "Take it, he doesn't like it anyway. We'll get it next time," but the truck in question was one of the host's favorites, so no such offer was possible. In retrospect—and in retrospect only—I've come to realize it was a good thing, because in my desperate state I would have accepted the truck, and set a Bad Precedent. With kids—and adults too, I guess—it's all about the Precedent. One morning you give your kid an Oreo so you can read more than the headlines, and from that day until your child goes to college, breakfast will be a battleground. *But yesterday you let me have a cookie.*

I've seen experienced mothers deal with toy grabs. In a calm yet firm voice they say, "That's so-and-so's toy. It will be here next time for us to enjoy. Let's go home and play with *your* trucks." And with that, the child loosens his grip and cheerfully heads home.

But although I would come to learn that voice, or to fake it, I hadn't as yet. I was still flashing stickers or fruit leather and whispering, "If you're good, I'll give this to you in the car," basically bribing my child to smooth our way out of every activity.

But I'd forgotten to bring my payola. All I had on me was the whisper, and this is what I chose to say, to a twenty-eight-month-old boy: "You don't want to be an unpleasant guest, do you? Your friend won't ask us back to his house."

The notion of being an unpleasant guest struck a chord. "I'm an unpleasant guest!" he yelled, lying on the floor and kicking. Not the chord I was hoping to strike.

As with the stock market, it's important to recognize when things are trending downhill and get out. Drenched in a sudden full-body sweat, I scooped him up and ran for the door.

So as not to repeat our mistakes in the future, should we be invited on another playdate again, I felt we should discuss what had gone wrong, but my partner fell asleep before we'd reached the end of the block. As he snoozed, I gazed at him in the rearview mirror and wondered where we should go from here, since despite his good looks (and intelligence and sparkle), we'd obviously blown this chance. Internet double dating? Maybe we could meet another couple in a Tonka truck chat room. Or perhaps a personal ad in the local parents' paper would be better: *SWT (that's T as in "toddler") seeks companionship. Do you like piña colada jelly beans? Let's jump on the bed together!*

Unfortunately, I'd talked up my big double date at the office, and because I've worked with the same group of women for about ten years, some of us (I won't name names, but "Sally" you know who you are) get insanely jealous when someone makes a new friend outside our insulated little ward.

One day one of the reporters announced to the group that she and her daughter were going on a playdate that afternoon, and that she really liked the other mother.

SALLY: "What's she like?"
REPORTER: "Really cool."

SALLY: "Be more specific. Does she have long legs?"

REPORTER: "Yes."

SALLY (obviously upset): "How does she dress?"

REPORTER: "Funky. She can carry off any look."

SALLY (fishing for a lifeline): "What's her hair like?"

REPORTER: "Nicole Kidman's."

SALLY (growing increasingly unhappy): "Does she rent or own?"

REPORTER: "They just bought. I guess her husband's really handy because she told me he's been doing a lot around the house."

SALLY: "Thanks a lot."

So as you can imagine, when I announced I'd Met Someone, I was grilled. They knew that She was originally from New York, just like me, and had been a journalist, and that our husbands were in similar fields, and so in a very schoolgirl fantasy way, it would have been SO PERFECT had it worked out. We would have sailed into the sunset behind a large construction site, where our boys could have watched backhoes and cement mixers and other vehicles I literally never saw until I had sons, although I guess they must have existed.

When I came to work the day after the date, my colleagues pounced.

"How'd it go?" Sally asked, obviously hoping for the worst.

From Here to Maternity

"Fine," I said, picking up a copy of the *Herald* and feigning interest in the sports section. But they know me too well to accept "fine," so they pushed until I finally confessed what had happened, and a veteran of the playdate world—her girls are twelve and nine—took my hand. "Oh well, dear," she said, "there are other mommies in the sea."

That was the last thing I wanted to hear. I wanted to talk to someone who would tell me that if something's meant to be, it won't be ruined so easily, someone who would say, "She'll call," and then when weeks passed without a call, offer excuses along the lines of "Maybe her child's sick," and then when I'd point out I knew her child wasn't sick because he went to school with my child, say, "Something must be going on with her, maybe she's sick." That's what I needed.

I couldn't stop myself from endlessly replaying the mistakes I'd made: "I shouldn't have confessed that usually I bribe my son," I told the group. "I think she was disgusted."

"Maybe you should play-date around," one of my coworkers said. "If you're busy, the time will pass faster." I knew it was good advice, because it's what I'd counseled another new mom who was involved in a toxic relationship with "Alexandra's" mother. They'd met a few months ago while dropping off their daughters at day care, but despite big talk about getting together, there was never any follow-up. The final straw was when Alexandra's mommy didn't return a phone call about a planned zoo outing. "Forget her," I told my friend. "I don't want to see you get hurt."

"I can't believe I care so much," she said, close to tears. "The next time I see her I'm going to act aloof."

But even years after graduating from high school, when you think you're over caring who's in the cool group, you realize that inside you're still sixteen. Helen recently moved into a new neighborhood, and after a few months in her dream home, she confessed that she spent a lot of time peeking through her window treatments to see who was playing with whom in the cul-de-sac. One day, her nightmare unfolded: her two next-door neighbors were out there together *with their children.* "I don't know if they just bumped into each other outside or if it was a planned thing," she said. "But I don't know why they didn't call me. My car was in the driveway so they knew we were home. I don't know whose feelings should be hurt," she added, "mine or [my daughter's]."

I sure understood how insecure she felt. Many mothers have told me they simply won't get their kids together with another child if they don't enjoy the other mom's company (or if she isn't a good contact).

A while ago, in a rare look at the touchy subject, the *New York Times* wrote about parental relations, noting that, "When it comes to budding friendships among children, sometimes the grown-ups can be more of a problem than the children." The *Times* story included a painful anecdote about a New York City mother who took her kindergartner to a playdate where the girl had fun, but the mom was an outcast. "Next time I'm sending the baby-sitter," she told the *Times*.

Well, I thought, *that* should send a message. In the unwritten playdate rules, sending a proxy is the ultimate slap. Here's a story that made the rounds of my local park. Two mothers had planned to get their kids together. The host mother bought new Play-Doh and made a nice fruit salad and even had her cleaning lady come a day early, only to open her door on the big day to see the child standing there with his . . . nanny.

That's right: the (would-be) hostess was stood up. Just who does the no-show mother think the playdates are for? The kids?

Please. Many of the children are so young they don't even notice who they're playing with (or next to, to be more precise). When you think about which member of the couple really needs companionship, it's the mom. But somehow the kids don't seem to understand that. I've been on countless playdates where the other mother and I are trying to chat, only to have the children interrupt us. Sometimes it's a snack request, or maybe a diaper needs to be changed.

One day, after months of talking about how we should get together, the writer who sits next to me at the *Herald* came over with her daughter. We'd been eager to chew over some delicious celebrity news, but between reading *Good Night, Gorilla* and monitoring the use of the allegedly washable markers, we had almost no time to ourselves.

"We'll have to talk tomorrow," she said. We'd both be working against tight midmorning deadlines, but a quarter of a million readers and a few impatient editors are nothing compared with the demands of two toddlers.

She and I had the luxury of chatting at work, but I don't work with most of the mothers I play-date, so frustrations build. Holly and I took the kids to music and art and gym classes, and went over to each other's houses, but in all those hours together we never really got to *talk*.

Finally, we couldn't take it anymore. "Let's go out to lunch," she said. "Just the two of us."

Alone at last, we sat down in a peaceful Japanese restaurant, and as we were enjoying the hot towels, pondering our sushi choices, and admiring each other's purses, she sighed. "It's so good to have a grown-up lunch." We settled in for a long conversation.

"So," she asked, "how are the kids?"

Chapter 13

A Snack Is a Terrible Thing to Waste (and a Waist Is a Terrible Thing to Lose)

I don't want you to get the wrong idea about me, but by this point you may be beyond persuading. I would never steal candy from a baby, not only because most babies don't actually have candy (they have those messy teething cookies and tasteless mashed peas), but even if they did have Twizzlers, I would respect basic rules of ownership.

However, the other day I found myself skulking in my kitchen, polishing off my children's animal crackers and chocolate milk, eating and drinking faster and faster as my little boys closed in on me. The depressing truth is that I see a difference between stealing candy from a baby and jacking a toddler's afternoon snack.

It was a damp November afternoon, the kind of day when you're glad to be inside and cozy, and my sons and I were reading *Harold and the Purple Crayon*. We were hanging out in their room, sitting on the floor surrounded by comfy pillows, and no one was trying to prevent his brother from seeing the illustrations or begging to be excused so he could go watch *Blue's Clues*. Anyone with children knows a bonding opportunity like this is not to be interrupted. Even if the house is burning down, you can wait a little. It takes a while for the fire department to arrive with the oxygen tanks and ladders, and for family members and news crews to assemble below with outstretched arms and lenses. And so, despite the fact that I was literally being tormented by the thought of those cookies and Nesquik just a few rooms away, I kept reading. An observer would have seen a mother and her children enjoying a classic children's story, and have no idea that the adult's mind was a cauldron of conflict. Still, I soldiered on, agreeing to read *Harold* "again, again" per my older son's request. That turned out to be my undoing. When we got to the part where Harold once again draws a picnic with "all nine kinds of pie that Harold liked best," I was overcome with emotion—and hunger.

But what to do? An earlier census of the cookie box had shown that three could not share in the meager provisions. Besides, I didn't want my kids to ruin their appetites. (I, on the other hand, should be so lucky as to ruin my appetite. My lifelong pursuit *has been* to ruin my appetite.) Explaining the situation to the boys was out of the question. "Let's

From Here to Maternity

all close our eyes for a moment and imagine we're in Harold's forest," I said cheerfully. The boys closed their innocent little eyes, and like a fugitive hoping to make it across the state line, I fled into the kitchen and began my feeding frenzy. I had barely wiped off the telltale chocolate milk mustache when I heard the heavy, uneven footsteps of the toddler cops.

"Mommy, where'd you go?" my older boy asked.

"Mommy had something she needed to do," I replied, attempting to pass off "guilt-ridden" as "authoritative." I wanted to have the kind of relationship where I'd feel comfortable showing my boys my weaknesses, but how could I explain to people who don't view stomach flu as a weight-loss opportunity—or who can leave half a brownie on their plates, and who allow themselves to be weighed *after* eating—that the cookies and the Nesquik had been calling me from the kitchen?

So there I was, caught, like some chain-gang escapee, and the only thought going through my mind was a prayer that, come dinner, I'd manage to keep my hands off the pizza I was planning to serve "them." And that's when a frightening thought hit me: losing the weight I'd gained during two rapid-fire pregnancies was nothing. While the "baby weight"* gets all the attention—*People* and *US* and

---

* As every pregnant woman knows, one of the first things they ask at your initial OB appointment is your "pre-pregnancy weight," or PPW. Ken was in the room when the nurse practitioner inquired about mine,

InStyle magazines run endless features on celebrities hiring personal trainers and chefs to help them shed extra pounds—it's actually easier to lose than toddler weight.

"Toddler weight?" you may be asking yourself. "Never heard of that." Me neither. I was so scared about baby weight that upon returning home from the hospital with my firstborn I immediately stripped down, slid the scale to a sympathetic spot on the bathroom floor, prepared myself for the worst, and hopped on. Subsequently, I followed my weight loss with the same level of interest with which I charted my new baby's progress, filling his/our baby book with pertinent information:

Four weeks: He follows me with his eyes; my Levi's went on but wouldn't zip

so I obviously faced a huge quandary. Long habit and his presence predisposed me to shave off a few pounds. But just as I was about to throw out a real lowball figure, I remembered that the number I gave would be used to set the bar for another important figure: my overall weight gain. The lower the weight I reported at the initial meeting, the more I'd "gain" during my pregnancy. Perhaps I should inflate my PPW, I thought. That way I could be one of those women you hear about—they become legends—who only put on twenty pounds.

On the other hand, pregnancy is the one time when women are *encouraged* to eat. "Go ahead, have a piece of cake," onlookers say, "you're eating for two." But bingeing when you're pregnant is like charging up a storm on your credit card. You can do it, but you're the same person who gets to pay the "bill" when it comes due.

What weight did I give the nurse? I'm not totally sure—they say the mind blacks out at traumatic moments—but I think that the two prospective lies met in the middle, and I actually told the truth. I say I'm not sure, because Ken knows me well enough to never bring up the subject again.

Six weeks: He's started to coo, and smile; the jeans zipped but wouldn't button

Two months: He grabs for objects; the jeans button, I'm grabbing for food

Seven months: He's starting to sit up; I really should get back to the sit-ups

After endless months of exercising and quasi-dieting (increasing the talk about dieting while decreasing the actual cutting back) I got within striking distance of my fighting weight . . . and then I got pregnant again, and repeated the weight gain and loss cycle, finally returning to the weight I was when I got married, not that I was so thrilled about it then, but everything's relative.

One of the more important things I still don't know, even after having two babies, is how long you get to lose your pregnancy weight. The lack of a ruling on this subject—from Joan Rivers, perhaps, or a distinguished panel of Condé Nast editors?—is particularly strange when you consider that the infant world is obsessed with time and deadlines. It takes nine months to make a baby. The American Academy of Pediatrics recommends mothers breastfeed for one year. If you wait fifteen days to make a return, the baby boutique in my neighborhood will only issue a merchandise credit. But how long does society grant you to lose your baby weight before you're no longer in a protected class? When do people have the right to gossip about you?

Not wanting to find out, I made sure to lose my baby weight fairly fast, so I thought I was all set—particularly because the rap on young kids is that they keep you thin. If I had a Fresca for every time I heard, "Running around after two boys must be the only diet you need"! I guess the "running" would have helped if the kids had done something productive, like race around a track. Alas, this mommy "running" is done within a one-foot radius, at home, near a refrigerator stocked with food for people who are trying to *grow.*

No one tells you this, but it's once the child's off Similac or breast milk, and on to macaroni and cheese, that your troubles start.

What's a mother to do? Any woman in her right mind (please judge me kindly here) knows she'd be safer living with a loaded gun in the house than a jar of Skippy Super Chunk, and yet, as a Good Mom, she's forced to serve food that contains actual caloric nutrition.

Which is why, more than a year after having my second child, I'm on what I've come to think of as the Mommy Diet. A mix of the tastiest elements of the South Beach Diet, Atkins, the Zone, and Weight Watchers, it's a high-fat, high-cal, high-tortellini-and-PB&J plan with lots of grapefruit and celery that never leave the fridge. It calls for snacking throughout the day—and eating six full meals. And the best/worst part about it? Dieting and maintaining are one and the same. And not only that, but unlike most diets, which have no wardrobe tie-ins, on the Mommy Diet your clothes practically choose themselves: the velour sweat suit, the relaxed-fit jeans, the men's button-down shirt.

The other day Helen and her daughter came over for the afternoon. Following appropriate playdate etiquette, I offered Helen tea or sparkling water, and served the children gingerbread men we'd made earlier (to impress some out-of-town visitors). Helen and I had our no-cal beverages. The kids had their homemade cookies . . . except that they were so busy playing with puppets and a new rocket that they didn't seem to notice the food, which was all that Helen and I could focus on.

"These couldn't be low-fat, could they?" she asked, reaching for a second. "You know how Weight Watchers tells you to write down everything you put in your mouth?" She bit off the gingerbread man's left arm and checked the fridge to see if we had any nonfat milk. "My list would be nine pages long—twenty grapes cut in half, a quarter of a stale plain bagel harvested from the car seat, two bites of a sodden grilled-cheese sandwich wolfed down just as I was about to scrape it into the safety of the garbage can, half a juice box of warm juice, six ounces of Stonyfield whole-milk yogurt, which by the way is way better than that low-fat stuff, two cold chicken nuggets, a gummed cheese stick, three raisins, the left arm of a gingerbread man . . ."

You don't hear much about it, but like grief, the Mommy Diet has five stages:

Denial: I'm just picking—these calories don't really count

Anger: Why am I gaining weight when I'm so careful all the time?

Bargaining: I'll lay off the grilled cheese if I can just go to the Barney's sale *alone*

Depression: I look like a middle-aged mother of two

Acceptance: I am powerless over Pepperidge Farm Goldfish

It's only now become clear to me how insidious the Mommy Diet is. You don't have to be anywhere near your children for it to be at work. How? Let me count the carb-ridden ways. 1) It's noon, and your coworkers are going down to the caf for lunch. Having risen at 4:30 with your one-year-old and breakfasted at 5:00, you've already eaten your lunch on the subway on the way to work, but eager for companionship, you join your colleagues, thereby adding a second midday meal to your repertoire. 2) It's 3:30 P.M., and in a self-pitying mood you "reward" yourself with an ice cream cone, or, unable to take a nap, you try to boost your energy with a sports bar. 3) It's Saturday night, you've been lucky enough to score a baby-sitter. What you'd really like to do is go to sleep, but because you're paying upwards of $10 an hour, you feel the need to make the evening special, and go out for a Big Dinner. 4) Your son's preschool is holding a bake sale and, being a generous mother, you need to make one batch for the sale and one for your son to have at home. 5) Or maybe you *are* with your child. He's playing a game where he feeds Mommy. Yelling "Get that cheese away from Mommy's mouth—she's not on Atkins anymore" does not send the child the right message.

As Helen and I watched the kids play and worked our way through the gingerbread men, we decided that gorging on kiddie food starts innocently enough. What harm could a Cheerio do? you ask, popping one into your mouth as you feed your baby one of his first solid foods. But just as recreational drinking can lead to a serious problem, Cheerios lead to Gerber's biter biscuits (only 45 calories per). From there it's jarred apricots (delicious over ice cream) and the next thing you know, you're making food for the kid that you know he doesn't want, or ordering him meals in restaurants just so you can eat the "leftovers." When you find yourself swigging whole milk out of the container at 7 A.M., you know you've hit bottom. No, wait. *Chocolate* milk is rock bottom.

A quick cautionary note about whole milk. As with other childhood foods that disappear from your diet as you age—peanut butter, macaroni and cheese, Chips Ahoys, potato puffs—any reunion is very dangerous. Kids' food is much better than ours. One day I made the mistake of mixing a little whole in with the skim for my Shredded Wheat 'N Bran and Toasted Oat Bran Squares. Yummm. Breakfast wasn't as punitive as usual. Day by day, I started tipping the whole/skim ratio until I was basically going through almost a quart of whole milk every few days. I'm not sure where it would have led—light cream? heavy cream? unsalted butter? lard? Luckily for me, Ken became concerned that *our kids* were drinking too much milk and maybe not getting enough nutrition from other sources.

"I'll talk to them," I said, silently vowing to wean myself from the good stuff.

Despite my best efforts, I still drink the kids' milk sometimes, but I am proud to report that I've never quaffed directly from a baby bottle, although I did start in on one of their sippy cups. But it wasn't my fault. We were driving home from gymnastics and the kids had fallen asleep without eating the snacks I'd packed for "them." Naturally I had to intervene—the honey wheat pretzels and Goldfish could go bad. That made me very thirsty, and while I obviously would have preferred Diet Coke to diluted orange juice, I didn't have any. I was forced to drink their juice, although of course there was no way to explain all this to the man idling next to me at the red light, who looked over, saw what was going down, and averted his eyes, as if he'd caught me belting out a show tune. I could tell he was scared.

I was scared, too. I'd never seen or even heard of another mother or father drinking from a child's cup. I had crossed some line. That night, when the kids were asleep and Ken was out buying emergency rations of three-cheese tortellini—it had become the only food my kids would eat but we kept running out because I liked it, too—I tried on a skirt that used to fit and looked at myself in the mirror. "My name is Mommy," I said, gasping for breath, "and I have a problem."

Chapter 14

Itty-Bitty Bioterrorism

When I say I have every known book on child health and safety, I'm not exaggerating. As you know, I share shelf space with a pediatrician. And yet none of them tells me what I need to know: If today is Tuesday, and Ken's mom has a cold, will she still be contagious on Saturday, when she and Ken's dad are planning to baby-sit, and I'm planning to shop for shoes to wear to a wedding we're—potentially—attending the very next day?

I hate to expose my babies to germs, and yet if I don't find sandals, or maybe a slingback, the only decent summer dress I have becomes unwearable, which means that unless it's unseasonably cold and I can get away with my red wool dress (which I do have shoes for), I'm in trouble.

Of course, I'm also in trouble if my kids catch Ken's mom's cold. You know how it goes. Both kids will get sick, but not at the same time, which, while painful, would at least allow me to serve my sentences concurrently. Instead, the back-to-back illnesses extend the period of combative nose-wiping, quarantine, and irritability (on my part) beyond what's healthy—mentally—for anyone involved. After a cold has blown through our family, I always say that if I ever let my boys go out again, they will be encased in those Ebola-safe suits the Hazmat teams wear.

As you can imagine, once I heard about Ken's mom's cold, I could think of little else—except the names of every baby-sitter in my own stable, and a few of those belonging to a couple of friends I was willing to sacrifice. On Wednesday, the doomsday clock ticking down, I awoke in a panic and dashed to my closet, hoping to find a wonderful pair of shoes I'd somehow forgotten, which would be current—or vintage—enough to wear to the wedding. But alas, nothing. I roused Ken. "You need to call your mom and see how she's feeling."

I was too nervous to listen in. But Ken's expression said the news from the other end wasn't good. "She's still stuffy," he reported. "Maybe you should plan on taking the kids to the zoo on Saturday instead of going shopping."

The zoo? How could my *alleged* soul mate be thinking about zebras—or the children and their little health concerns—at a time like this? Everyone knew that at the wedding all eyes would be on me—a random guest—and her footwear.

But Ken, being a man of science, a man who understands complicated matters like germ transmission, a man who believes that black patent-leather sandals could work (!) with a brown floral dress, a man who, because he had to work all day in the ER on Saturday wasn't facing the cancellation of *his* trip to Saks, wanted to play it safe.

As for me, the person embedded with two toddlers who are terrible shoppers, I saw the problem this way: Why forsake a definite four-hour shopping trip for only the *potential* of possibly avoiding a cold? As the wedding drew closer, I became less and less risk-averse. By Thursday evening, still empty on both the shoe and backup baby-sitter fronts, I had become so shortsighted that if Typhoid Mary herself was available, and was willing to watch two boys under the age of three years old, I would have welcomed her into my home. "The diapers are in the top drawer, there's string cheese in the fridge, and try not to breathe on the kids."

On Friday morning, with Ken's mom still reporting some congestion, a ray of light shone through. You know those stories about mothers—size 4—petite—who lift a Hummer to free a toddler from beneath the front axle? A starving woman who feeds her own rations to her babies but wills herself to stay alive so she can care for her kids? Well, this was my moment. I was unloading sippy cups from the dishwasher and methodically sticking the valves in the tops—it's replaced the morning news shows in my A.M. routine—when I had an epiphany regarding infectious disease. "Wait a minute!" I called out to Ken. I had just remembered that the kids had been riding out the tail end of their own colds when they visited Ken's parents the previous weekend, so my mother-in-law's immutable cold was not really hers, but . . . *theirs*. Which meant that according to the rules of immunity, not only wouldn't the kids re-catch it, but neither would Ken or I. "Tell your parents I'll drop the boys off at three," I said. "Sharp."

The good doctor was impressed with my logic, but he still wanted a little something that the *New England Journal of Medicine* and the *Journal of the American Medical Association* would consider publishable. In *my* peer-reviewed journals—*Vogue, Glamour, Cosmo*—a convincingly stated and convenient hypothesis such as I had just posited would have been more than enough. When shoes are at stake, My People know better than to look too deep. *What? There's a sale at Stuart Weitzman and you have no child care except the nine-year-old who lives upstairs? Just give her your cell number and go.*

As disappointed as I was that Ken didn't want to close his eyes and hope for the best on Saturday, the thought that we might be losing four hours of baby-sitting for absolutely no reason did inspire him.

"What we need," he said, "is rapid viral subtyping."

He imagined an at-home test, much like the pregnancy tests, that would determine the pedigree of the illness that's threatening to derail your life. The subject would smear mucus on your silk blouse, and the sample would be rushed to your bathroom for insta-analysis. If luck was running your way, the lab tests would show that this was not some new cold, but rather the very one that ripped through your household two weeks ago. It couldn't hurt you a second time.

Brilliant, right? That's what I thought, and its genius was confirmed by a focus group I assembled the next day. "Imagine how it would change your life," one of the members said, a dreamy look in her eyes. Unlike a serious illness, when your concern is for the child, the common cold is widely known to inflict more of a hardship on the mother. Allison, who ranks sickness by the discomfort not to the patient, but to the parent, considers ear infections the "best." When I expressed surprise—"But they're so painful!"—she said, "Yeah, that's true, but they're not communicable. You can still visit people."

In the end, it all comes down to the ability to get out of the house, to *visit*, as anyone with kids knows. But, just as with a game of phone tag, where the two parties involved can go for weeks without managing to talk, so can two well-meaning mothers never pull off a playdate. First one child gets sick. The period during the actual illness is blacked out, of course, as is some undefined post-illness, the "just to be safe" phase. Once this ends, a sibling, or a child from the other family involved, will come down with something, and another rain delay will be called.

Depending on the decision makers' paranoia level, the children may not meet until they're adults, and what could have been a beautiful friendship that started in the nursery—"We've known each other since we were in diapers," they'd later tell their spouses—is nipped before the bud. Or, even worse, a marriage between the son of one friend and the daughter of another never happens because their moms were too germophobic to let the would-be sweethearts play, and twenty-eight years later each child marries someone with dull parents, who mar every extended-family get-together.

I know I shouldn't admit this, but sometimes, even if a runny nose has been confessed, or the word "cough" whispered, I'll go ahead with the playdate. Like a NASA mission-control specialist deciding whether to launch a shuttle, I factor several variables into the decision. In descending order, they are: how much I like the other mother; how much tussling is going on at my house at the moment; what kind of food we have at home; and—wait, there's something I'm forgetting. Oh yeah: how sick the other kid is.

But unfortunately, regarding playdate decisions, not everyone is willing to consider the mother's clinical need to talk to someone whose idea of conversation extends beyond what the pig says. Some mothers follow illness-reporting requirements that would satisfy the Centers for Disease Control.

I was faced with one of these really annoying full-disclosure situations the other day. Having tired of thousands of dollars' worth of puzzles, books, and trains, and enough construction vehicles to tear down and rebuild Boston, my children and I were psyched to socialize. I was packing the diaper bag and filling sippy cups and making sandwiches for our fifteen-minute car ride when the phone rang. It had the ring of the 7 P.M. call from your husband when he's supposed to be home at 7 P.M.

Maybe, I thought, crossing my fingers, the other mom is calling because she wants to serve ice cream, or wheat-based products (oh, please let it be homemade chocolate chip cookies!) and wants to make sure neither of my kids is lactose- or Toll House–intolerant. Yeah, about as likely as Mary Poppins herself showing up at my door on Saturday.

"Just so you know," she began, "Tom had a cold *three weeks ago*. He's better, but he's still sniffling, but that may just be allergies. I should also tell you that someone in Anna's day care had some kind of fungus. She hasn't caught it, so I don't think it's in our home, but . . ."

Too much information is rarely a good thing. Against my better judgment, I'd been playing up the excursion for the past three hours, and if it were to be called off, I was going to have to come up with an acceptable substitute activity, something they'd truly enjoy, like crossing the highway without holding my hand, or resetting the TiVo to record a car race instead of the movie I wanted to see. But how in good conscience could I take my children into a home the World Health Organization would have quarantined? If they came down with something, I wouldn't even have righteous indignation on my side, which is almost as useful as Infant Motrin.

In the same way it's always the cover-up—not the underlying crime—that gets people in trouble, responsibility for an illness can become more important than the illness it-self. In even the best relationships there's a subtle, unspoken accounting that goes on at all times. With a friend it can be something like "Let's see, I listened to you complain about your ex-husband for two years, so not a word about my whining for a while" or "You had us over for dinner six times last year, compared with our four, so let me get lunch today." In the case at hand, if I knowingly and willingly took our children into an environment teeming with dis-ease, Ken would be the one socking away credits he could redeem next time.

Opposite the moms who list every illness everyone in their extended circle has contracted or simply heard about, are the moms who feign ailment ignorance—the bioterror-ists. Their kids can have bilateral pinkeye with gallons of green discharge, a fever of 102 degrees Fahrenheit, and oc-casional vomiting, yet when they show any symptoms dur-ing our shared time, the mom acts surprised.

For example: The kids and I had driven over to Allison's for a playdate, and we were standing outside the door, re-viewing what it means to be a good guest, when a loud hacking cough echoed from inside. Was the TV tuned to a documentary about coughing codes during World War II? Had the dog swallowed a fishbone?

I had my answer soon enough. It was Allison's son.

Being a litigator, Allison's first impulse was not to com-fort her child or offer the little boy some water, but to deny prior knowledge: "He just started coughing, I swear," she said, slapping the kid on the back, as if that would help. When her son started sneezing, Allison changed strategy and threw herself upon my mercy. "*Please* don't tell Ken," she pleaded.

Like a lot of my friends, Allison takes comfort in having a pediatrician who, without laughing, takes around-the-clock requests such as: "I'm afraid to cut the baby's nails. Can I bring him over so you can do it?" Understandably, Allison didn't want to do anything to turn Ken against her, like, ahem—I mean achoo!—getting his children sick.

As for me, I was in the mood to hang out, and definitely not in the mood to assume responsibility. "Don't worry," I said, accepting hush money in the guise of Godiva. And besides, at least she had the good manners to feel guilty about the situation. I'd definitely take her remorse into account when my kids caught her son's illness.

But there are moms who see nothing wrong with exposing your children to their kid's germs. One morning I was walking out of my older son's preschool with such a person. "I'm glad Hannah let me leave without crying," she said. "She's been sick all week and really clingy. She gets like that when she's feverish."

Sick all week? Really clingy? Feverish?

Because this devastating news was delivered in the same tone that you'd use to report that your child will only wear light-up sneakers, or refuses all food that's not red, at first I wasn't sure I'd heard her correctly. But when it became clear that I had, I was panicked. Do I dash into the classroom as if it were a pit of fire, grab my son, and run him to safety? Find a distant pay phone, cover the mouthpiece with a cloth, and rat Hannah out? Appealing as that last option was, it smacked of poor sportsmanship. In the end, I put myself in Fate's hands.

Which is the same approach I was about to suggest we take with Ken's mom. You know how you always remember where you were when you received important news? Years from now, I'm sure I'll recall that I was on the StairMaster at the gym when my cell phone rang that Friday evening. I could see from the caller ID that it was Ken, and since I'd just left him fifteen minutes earlier, and he knew my gym enforced a strict no-cell policy, I didn't think he was calling to chat. Perhaps he had a question regarding the where-abouts of clean pajamas for the kids? (Answer: at the store.)

"My mother's recovered," he reported. "Her cold's gone."

I stopped reading *Oprah* and started dreaming about my Saturday afternoon. Maybe Helen could come with me, and we could hit both Saks and Lord & Taylor, and then go for a post-shoe California roll . . . and that's when a dark thought intruded on my fantasy.

Ken's dad.

What if he had caught The Cold and was poised to start showing symptoms on Saturday afternoon, just as we were about to head over? Subpoena-dodging measures were nec-essary. My plan was to snip the land lines, hide the cell phones, and leave the laptop at work. Then, come Saturday, having been incommunicado for the entire morning, I'd drive to my in-laws, slow the car down, remind my older son how to ring his grandparents' doorbell, and then *gently and safely* push the kids out onto the soft lawn. Then peel away.

I know it sounds extreme but, sincerely, I was only thinking of my boys. They so enjoy spending time with their grandparents.

Chapter 15

Mother's Little Helper

I let my kids watch TV. Actually, I don't just *let* my kids, I encourage it. I push it.

Like many hard truths, I hadn't realized this until one morning when I heard myself saying—well, I'll get to that hard truth soon enough. Here's the soft story part: I (was) awakened at 5:30 A.M., which should have made it quite easy to leave the house by 8:30, but three hours is both too much and too little time to get a pair of toddlers out the door. If you diaper and dress them too early, you'll just have to repeat the sequence, *Groundhog Day* style, right before it's time to go. Wait too long, and you'll find yourself frantically stuffing little hands into jacket arms and saying "If we don't hurry, we're going to hit rush-hour traffic" to people who don't even own watches.

My goal was to have completed the inevitable turtleneck-and-socks-and-shoes struggles by 8:10, which would allow me time to groom and dress myself before the pre-school and playgroup drop-offs. (At work, everyone already knows I'm a schlump, but the mothers of my kids' school-mates were a new audience.) Although my children hap-pened to be playing happily with their trains at the moment, one had just hit two-berty and the other had just left it, so I knew this activity was a ticking time bomb, and soon enough a dispute would erupt over a bridge trestle or Gordon, a particularly prized train in the Thomas line. I needed to interest them in a less-charged pastime if I wanted to make it through the two-minute cycle on my electric toothbrush, among other indulgences.

In other words, I needed TV. Mother's little helper.

"Who wants to watch *Caillou*?" I asked, not so ashamed of myself that I was prevented from hunting for the remote and calling up a TiVo'd episode. At the mention of their beloved's name, the kids abandoned their creative play and plopped themselves in the mini director's chairs in front of the TV, starting down the path toward a life of obesity sim-ply because their mother wanted to brush her teeth and blow-dry her hair. Consoling myself that they'd get exercise and stimulation at school, I headed into the bathroom for twenty minutes of me-time, but moments later I heard my younger son approaching. "I need koss," he said, pointing to the dental floss.

I pulled off a length of floss that I hoped was too short to be a strangulation hazard, and too long to be easily swal-

Mother's Little Helper   153

lowed, and I steered him back toward the television, playing up the action on the screen. "Oh, look, Caillou's in the park," I said. But my older son was no longer in the mood for Caillou. "I want to go *now*," he said, heading toward the front door, which he's fully capable of unlocking and opening, the better to provide his younger brother with access to the apartment building's two-flight staircase.

"We can't go," I said, standing there in my bathrobe, "I'm not ready yet."

"Why not?" he asked.

For a moment I considered giving him a real answer, explaining that since having children I hadn't really gotten enough sleep, and my skin had suffered, so I needed to make sure that at least my hair looked good, and, in addition, I had let my wardrobe dwindle, and with fewer things I like, dressing takes longer. But I feared the truth might be lost on someone who doesn't even glance in the mirror after a haircut. "I can't go out in my bathrobe," I said. "That would be silly."

One thing I've learned about managing toddlers—and there may be only this one thing—is the power of the word "silly." Just as many adults blindly accept "Insurance purposes" as an explanation, toddlers buy "It would be silly." Without a fight, my older son dutifully returned to *Caillou*. But I knew the flimsy plot wasn't going to hold his attention. Something stronger was called for. "I think *Dragon Tales* is on," I said, reassuring myself that as worthless as the show may be, it *is* at least on PBS, so if the three of us happened to be abducted from the house while it was play-ing, police scouring the crime scene would report that we'd been watching educational TV.

With the clock ticking down, I jumped in the shower, only to hear the horrifying pitter-patter of little feet, fol-lowed by the sound of my younger son climbing on my bed. "No jumping," I called out over the spray. I heard his brother join him and the bed springs start to squeak. "No more monkeys jumping on the bed," I sang out, trying to do what I thought Mary Poppins would do, in the extremely unlikely event she found herself in a similar situation.

More jumping. "Maybe *Barney* is on," I said. Continued jumping. "Or *Teletubbies*."

Pathetically, I knew the kiddie TV morning lineup well enough to know that *Teletubbies* and *Barney* most certainly were *not* on. *Tweenies*, sort of a *Barney* Lite, if you can imagine that, was screening at the moment. But I figured I'd lure them to the TV and hope they'd fall under its spell once in range. Dripping wet, and trying not to ruin the hardwood floors, I hopped from rug to rug as I corralled them back to the living room, only to discover that the screen, once alive with joy and animation, had gone dark.

"OK," I said, sounding like a ruthless detective (not the loving, intellectual mother-trying-to-do-the-best-for-her-two-sons-at-all-times that I really am), "who turned off the TV?"

The children looked nervous. "He did," my older son said, pointing.

Mother's Little Helper   155

I would have dusted for prints or pulled out my home polygraph machine, but what good would finding the culprit do me anyway? How do you punish a child who doesn't want to watch TV? Make him watch it? (For that matter, how do you punish a child who loves TV? Turning it off hurts you as much as it does him, maybe more.)

Where did I go wrong? I wondered as I dried myself off and settled for a pair of Gap jeans that I'd once loved but could no longer stand. I was thinking about a study that had been released just a few days earlier. It found that 59 percent of children aged six months to two years watch television, and 42 percent watch videotapes or DVDs. And not only that, but the median time they spend watching some form of media is slightly more than two hours per day. Two hours. And here my kids are, turning *off* the machine. Maybe I should set up a reward system, I thought. Give them a toy sword for every half hour watched. Or we could take a Mommy, Me, and TV class, if one existed, but of course one never would, because letting a child watch TV, not to mention teaching a child to watch TV, is one of the worst crimes a parent can commit.

Even TV itself makes you feel guilty. Like the alcohol companies, even as it's pushing its product, it's suggesting that you not imbibe—or, if you *must*, that at least you do so responsibly. Here's an example of this kind of guilt trip. Target is a PBS sponsor, and the chain's promotional spots show a beautiful woman reading to a circle of adorable children. "Read to children," the voiceover says, "so kids can read." That line—"so kids can read"—is often the last thing I hear as I leave my kids in front of the boob tube as I head into the kitchen to make dinner.

But Target's goody-two-shoes act can be written off as crass marketing efforts. More painful, because it lacks a financial motive and might actually be a good idea, is the American Academy of Pediatrics' recommendation that kids under two watch no television at all. The AAP came up with this brilliant idea in 1999, the year after *Teletubbies* invaded America.

Most mothers don't like to talk about the AAP's zero-tolerance policy, but it came up in conversation after I'd confessed I'd turned on my kids for turning off the TV; one mother explained that it would be "dangerous" to keep her children from the TV. "They'd be running around in rags starving to death," she said. Albeit with a complete and laudable ignorance of *Teletubbies*.

If the AAP is going to issue high-minded proclamations like that, it should be required by federal law to dispatch member pediatricians prepared to read, glue, and play finger-puppet games as early as 5:30 A.M. Then we'll see who considers TV such a bad influence.

Either that, or we could change a few things, namely how television time is calculated. In the New Mommy Math, half an hour on an educational station (PBS, Disney, Noggin, E!, or Lifetime), or any DVD containing the words "Einstein," "genius," "brainy," or "Mozart," counts as fifteen minutes toward your child's daily media tally. Mommy

Math tallies only the time the child is *actually* watching the show. An eight-second snippet of attention does not count as a whole minute as it does on your cell phone bill. Time spent fighting with a sibling is not calculated, nor is time spent in Mommy's room while she's trying to get ready.

Further, if Mom watches the show with her child and illuminates or in any way expands upon the on-screen action—"Dora's crossing a bridge!"—she gets "clean air credits" in the form of a minute-for-minute bonus. Additionally, if the child dances or sings along with the on-screen characters, or plays along with any games taking place on the show, the program does not count as TV at all, but rather as Montessori.

Lastly, any baby-sitter caught using up the kid's daily allowance on her watch, and hence cutting into the time when the child could be watching while *you're* on duty, has to work an extra hour, for free, and *read* to the child the whole time.

But even as I'm proposing the New Mommy Math, I'm feeling guilty, because admitting that you let your child watch TV (not to mention forcing it on him) is tantamount to saying "I think reading's for the birds." (Birds, on the other hand, make for a terrific nature channel if you have a picture window—and that doesn't count as TV.)

"But if you don't let your kids watch TV, they won't recognize the characters all of their friends are talking about," my mom said when I told her I was upset because my older son, in addition to being able to identify any show just by

hearing the first note of the theme song, recently spontaneously sang out "PBS Kids!"—in public.

"You shouldn't worry so much about everything," my
mother said. But it's hard not to. Because despite the statis-
tics I mentioned earlier—the ones showing that kids watch
a lot of TV—only *one* of my friends freely admits that her
kids spend any time at all in front of the tube. Here's her
(overly convenient) theory: "There's a lot of lying going
on," she said. "It's like McDonald's shame. *No one* lets their
kids eat at McDonald's, but—surprise! Everyone has enormous collections of Happy Meals toys.

"It's such a charged issue," she added. She and her husband have been filling out private-school applications, and
all asked about TV consumption. "We didn't know how
much to put down," she said, the truth obviously not being
an option. "None? That wouldn't be credible, but I sense
they have some formula; if we admit to an hour a day
they'll figure that's three." ("Occasionally," she speculated,
means all day long.)

Actually, her children do not watch much TV. "But for
the wrong reasons," she explained. "In a perverse way, I'm
trying to make it more powerful, so when it's on, they're
glued."

"What's the sweet spot?" I asked. "How much can you
let them watch a day without making it commonplace?"

Alas, she had not yet figured out the answer.

The problem with lying about TV viewing habits is
that, by necessity, your child is your partner in crime, and

from my experience these are not people you can rely on to keep a secret. Heck, even many adults, ashamed of watching a show like *Melrose Place* or *Dawson's Creek*, often inadvertently reveal their true viewing habits by showing a little too much interest in the morning-after office discussion of a program they supposedly don't watch. I still remember the reaction of a coworker who insisted he'd never seen *Sex and the City* when he learned in the cafeteria that Carrie was planning to move to Paris with the Russian. "Are you kidding me?" he practically shouted. "What about her column and her apartment?"

Imagine coaching your two-year-old: *OK, if Barney's name is ever mentioned, pretend you think they're talking about the store, and then act confused when someone mentions a purple dinosaur or says "Baby Bop."*

But good luck trying to pull it off. I was at the park a while ago with a mother who had previously told me, very proudly, that her kid watched no TV, when, as if to test her assertion, a three-year-old boy wearing a "Bob the Builder" costume showed up. Although his tool belt and construction helmet were very rinky-dink, all of the children acted as though a rock star had descended on the park. Mobbing him from all directions—vacating the swings and the slide and the see-saw—they broke into lyrics. "Bob the builder/Can we fix it?/Bob the builder/Yes we can!" *Her son included.* "He must have seen it at a friend's house," she said.

Or, to give her the benefit of the doubt, he might have been infected with Bob at preschool. Like the most successful germs, Bob is passed along quite easily—the mere sight of a bag of eponymous graham crackers can do it. And, like secondhand smoke, secondhand Bob—or Dora or Maisy—can be hazardous to Mom's carefully constructed image. One day, one of my friends proudly told me that her son had created an "imaginary vehicle," a "zooper car." "I don't know how he came up with that one," she said. I didn't either, until a month later when I was watching *George Shrinks* for the first time, and what should George's main method of transport be? I won't spoil the surprise, in case you have a very creative child, too.

I didn't break the news to my friend, and hopefully she'll go to her son's Nobel Prize ceremony still proud that her boy made up his own vehicle when he was a toddler. I'd love a delusion like that. When my younger son was about eighteen months old he would wrap his arms around his big brother and say, "big hug." It was the sweetest thing I'd ever seen—and I told everyone I knew about it—until the day I saw two of the Teletubbies embracing and squeaking the words "big hug." It was almost enough to make me turn off the TV.

Almost.

But as bad as it is to admit you let your child watch television, there's nothing, absolutely nothing worse than being caught in the act. One day, one of my older son's friends was coming over to play, and I wanted to clean the apartment before his guest arrived. Although my kids like to help vacuum and wipe the walls with paper towels, their assistance is better when time is not of the essence, and cleaning is not the actual object.

TV was called for. I should have timed things better, or dead-bolted the door, but just as I was fishing a sippy cup from underneath the couch, the doorbell rang, and before I could run across the apartment and turn off the *Blues Clues* video, my older son flung open the door to reveal, for all the world to see, a televised Steve strumming his guitar and singing "The Good-bye Song."

I'd rather be caught with liquor on my breath midday than be snagged with the television on before prime time, but it was too late for regrets. The question was, *Where should I go from here?* I appeared to be—and in fact, was— a mother who not only let her kids watch TV during the day, but was so far gone she didn't even have the decency to be ashamed enough to conceal her actions.

"Oh, hello!" I chirped, considering my options: 1) Pretend the TV was stuck on the On position; 2) Claim I was doing research for a column; 3) Offer gin and Marlboros all around, so the TV would seem like the least of our problems.

Or perhaps I could tell the truth: "I'm teaching them to watch TV, and this is simply part of our lesson plan. We're ready for a break now, come on in."

Chapter 16

True Lies

I'd like to tell you that there was a legitimate reason why I didn't take my children trick-or-treating on Halloween (criminals always have their excuses). I could explain that Ken was working in the ER that night, which meant I'd be alone, and I was worried about managing two frisky astronauts by myself on a busy street, particularly since I was in a highly agitated state, given all the candy at stake. But that doesn't really make it any better, does it?

The thing is, I almost got away with it, too. It was 6:50 P.M. on October 31, and my children, little geniuses that they are, were nonetheless blissfully unaware that the biggest day of the kiddie calendar was upon us, or, I should say, upon everyone else. We'd gone to a Halloween party a few days earlier, and as far as they knew, Halloween was a holiday celebrated midmorning *inside*, with traditional foods such as apples and tofu ice cream sandwiches. And I certainly wasn't about to clue them in on the truth—I convinced myself I was hustling bedtime along for their sake (they're so much happier when they're well rested, aren't they?). But I also had a new issue of the *Atlantic* waiting for me.

Having accomplished dinner and the bath without incident—well, there were three incidents actually, but as Ken noted the other day, between 0 and 3 incidents is the new "none"—I was ready to put my younger son to bed, and thereby inch that much closer to relaxation, when the doorbell rang. Like a dog hearing the bath water running in the guest bathroom when there's no company staying over, I knew the buzzer was not good news.

I flashed back to my training: a few weeks after my older son was born, Ken invited a nurse over to the house to teach me and some new-mom friends what to do in various pediatric emergencies. The buzzer rang again. "Just remember ABC," she'd instructed, holding a life-sized baby doll and demonstrating how to revive a child. "Airway. Breathing. Circulation."

"Airway. Breathing. Circulation," I repeated calmly that Halloween night. I was starting to congratulate myself for staying cool in a life-threatening situation, when I remembered that no one was choking on a sour ball or having an allergic reaction to a Mr. Goodbar. And how could they be? They hadn't been trick-or-treating. I would have paged the nurse and whispered my query into the phone: "What do you do when you've concealed Halloween from your kids, and costumed children are starting to show up at your door?" But the buzzer rang a third, long time.

I could have ignored it, but who knows what a modern rebuffed trick-or-treater might do? Steal my identity? Unleash a computer virus on my home network? "I'll get the door, you guys stay here!" I said. I tried to sound casual, but they smelled fear. Although they'd both been getting kind of mellow, at the prospect of a visitor they perked right up. "Who is it, Mommy?"

Like I could tell them the truth. I let a pink princess into the vestibule and indicated that she should stay put, at all costs. Her mother, peeking around the corner, must have wondered what all the gesticulating was about, but I wanted to make sure the girl didn't poke her head into the apartment. There could be no contact between Cinderella and my boys. "I'll be right back," I said, dashing to the kitchen for my stash of Milky Ways. As I reached into the cabinet, I heard my kids greeting our little dignitary.

Older son: "I was an astronaut for Halloween."

Princess (apparently baffled by his use of the past tense, as not only was she old enough to know that *today* was the holiday, but she obviously came from a family whose mother was comfortable enough in the world to observe Halloween): "Halloween's today."

As if trying to break up a political conversation between friends of different beliefs, I ran over and inserted myself between them. I thought I'd successfully blocked my boys' view of her plastic pumpkin as I jammed in the candy, but I guess I didn't. "I want teet," my younger said. "That's how he says 'treat,' " I translated for the pink princess, who headed off on her rounds, unaware of the devastation she'd left in her wake.

I looked at my watch. A mere three minutes had elapsed, but they were going to cost me, in triplicate. Minimum. Sort of like punitive damages. Unable to hold off the pleas for a "teet," I agreed to hand one over, but there was no way I was introducing Milky Ways—or, as I thought of them, "fun-sized" caffeine delivery systems—at that hour. "You can each have a vanilla cookie," I heard Monster Mom saying. "And then it's bedtime." As I brought out two plates, each holding a lone apple juice—sweetened wafer, my thoughts turned glum. So desperate for a few moments alone at the end of the day, I'd come to the point where I was denying my boys one of childhood's best rites. And I'd once considered myself a fun person! Usually when I feel this way I call a friend for reassurance that "everyone does that." But all of my friends were out trick-or-treating with their kids. Some reassurance.

With no one to talk to, I got down to business. I'd deal with my guilt twinges later—during the time I'd been planning to read. "I love you so much," I told my younger son as I carried him into his room. I was sneaking away from his crib when the doorbell rang again. In a horror flick, not only would I have been wearing heels and showing more décolletage, but the audience would have been screaming "Don't answer the door!" Unfortunately, with my dwindling free time at stake, this was scarier than the movies.

When I got to the living room my older son was looking out the window at three Power Rangers. Aware that time was my enemy, I grabbed some candy and rushed outside. Who knows what kind of joy he would have spotted there? Incredibly, he stayed put—but that didn't mean he wasn't curious. "What did you give them?" he asked when I returned. *Does he have X-ray vision?* I wondered as I began my lie. "Vitamins," I said, trying to staunch the larger issue: "Why are children we don't know coming to our door and getting vitamins?" Handing over an orange Wilma (and wondering how the Flintstones have managed to retain dominance in the vitamin world despite the fact that children today don't even know who they are), I swept him off to bed, telling him his favorite story, in which he's "the best astronaut in the country" and NASA needs him to fly an important mission to the moon. At least he could dream about being an astronaut, I thought—and with no worries about tooth decay.

The next day, my head pounding with a guilt hangover, I confessed what I'd done—*not* done—in my *Herald* column, and when it ran I was heckled all day by colleagues, to the point where I needed a pick-me-up, so I called my hairdresser. When I gave my name, the guy doing the schedul-

ing gasped. "You didn't tell your children it was Halloween!" he said. "*That* will be something for your kids to
talk about on the couch."

Before having kids I'd heard people say things like that
but I'd never given the matter much thought. Now I give it
much thought all the time, as do most of my friends. "I'm
thinking of putting them in therapy now so they can start
to work on what I've done in real time," Dana said. She told
me a Christmas tale:

Her kids wouldn't stop fighting with each other. Finally
(after about three minutes) she could take it no longer. "I
went upstairs into my office and called our home number,"
she said. She ran downstairs and answered it. "Oh, hello,
Mrs. Claus," she said into the phone. Mrs. Claus was on the
line? Her children stopped bickering and snapped to attention. "Yes, they *have* been fighting. Oh? Santa's not going to
give them any toys?" Her son started to cry. "What if they
start being good now? It's already too late? Couldn't he at
least give them one present each?" Her daughter started to
cry. "Yes? But not the train and the doll house?"—their two
top requests. "OK, I'll tell them to be good from now on so
next Christmas will be better."

Her children were too young to have their own shrinks
at that point, so Dana told *her* therapist about what she'd
done. "He gave a bemused smile," she said. "It was sort of a
'Don't make a habit of it' response. I was prepared for him
to say, 'How did you feel after you did that?' or 'What made
you think that was the right way to handle the situation?'

Then I would have explained that lying was the lesser of two evils. Either lie, or flee the house leaving the two of them locked in a duel to the death."

No one who lies to a child wants to—children force you into it. Allison convinced me of this. At her son's third birthday party, twenty-five children all brought gifts—which Allison practically ripped out of their hands upon entry. "I didn't want Sam to see them," she confessed later. I thought back to the party and recalled our gift being snatched before we'd even said hello. At the time I thought Allison was suffering from typical mother-of-the-birthday-child jitters. I'd been to her toy-filled house before, so I knew she wasn't trying to instill an antimaterialist spirit in the boy. "Well," she said sheepishly, "once they're opened, you can't return them or re-gift them." She stopped abruptly. The white elephant in the conversation was obviously my gift—an endangered-species puzzle—and who would be getting it next. "We kept your present," she added quickly. "It was wonderful."

(When I mentioned the story to Ken, he said, "She'd better start a massive database to prevent the most dreaded of all the re-gifting errors: giving the gift back to the person who gave it to you." We considered installing radio frequency IDs in all our future gifts—not to snag re-gifters, but so we could conduct our own satisfaction surveys by tracking our gifts' progress through the birthday party circuit. *Let's see now, Mr. Potato Head made four stops before he finally landed for good at the Stevensons' house, but Candy Land stuck on its very first stop.*)

"Didn't Sam wonder why he didn't get any presents?" I asked.

"I was really worried about that," Allison admitted, "but he didn't say anything. But I was punished anyway. Imagine how terrible I felt writing the thank-you notes, in one case for a present I'd already given away. But I did it for Sam. I want him to be able to give other kids nice presents—to seem generous—but he gets invited to so many parties . . ."

Well, at least Sam had his own party. I heard about one mom who took her son to another child's party—their birthdays were three days apart—and told him *that* was his party. "Wasn't he curious why no one sang 'Happy Birthday' to him when the cake came out?" I asked. My friend didn't know. I guess even very young children sense when something is too weird to get into.

Except when they don't sense it. When Dana came home from the hospital with her second child she told me that she was "at the start of a six-month lie" (her entire maternity leave). On the first day home from the hospital, her husband took their daughter to preschool, and she asked why he wasn't wearing a suit (this is the kind of thing the daughter of a fashion devotee notices). "Without thinking," Dana said, "he explained he was wearing jeans because he was heading back home to help with the new baby." The new big sister took in the information. "I want to stay home too," she declared. Uh-oh. Dad still had a few days left on his paternity leave, but for the rest of the week he dressed

From Here to Maternity

up for the drop-off so she'd think he was heading into the office. "I guess he could have pretended his office was going casual," Dana said, "but that's too big of a lie—everyone knows the whole Dockers and sweaters thing is over." I asked what she'd do once her husband went back to work and *she* started taking her daughter to school. "I'll have to put on heels," she said. "I'll be like one of those husbands you hear about who's lost his job but doesn't tell his wife, and leaves the house each morning pretending to go to work."

When I pointed out that, yes, she was lying, but it was a white lie meant to save her daughter's feelings, she quickly set me straight. "Her feelings have nothing to do with it," she said, as she breast-fed her one-week-old and tried to keep her jealous mutt at bay. "I'm joking—sort of."

"Well," I said, "at least you don't hide from her when she *is* home." I was thinking about some stories I'd heard (and told) at a cocktail party I'd gone to a few nights earlier. The hostess was giving a bunch of us a tour of her new home, and confessed that she sometimes hides out from her toddler (when he's with his nanny). "I hear him calling me, 'Mama, Mama, Mama,' " she said, "but I duck into the den or the library and close the door." She occasionally calls the nanny's cell phone from her room if she needs to tell her something and doesn't want her son to know she's home.

As she spoke, the three other women in the conversational circle were doing that thing where you're not so much listening as composing your own anecdote. (As Fran

Lebowitz famously observed, "The opposite of talking isn't listening. The opposite of talking is waiting.") I admitted that several times during the past summer I'd made a big show of leaving through the front door, only to sneak back in through the back door and head up to the deck, where I'd set up my laptop out of sight of my own flesh and blood. And once, when my mom and I were walking down the street and I spotted the kids and the baby-sitter coming toward us on their way back from the park, I grabbed her arm and yanked her down a side street. "You're like an illegal alien fleeing the INS," she observed. When I finished telling my stories, another mom confessed that she'd scurried up a ladder into a crawl space when she heard her daughter coming into her room, and the third woman told us that she'd once left for the gym without her sneakers, sports bra, or shorts, but didn't go back into the house to get them. "I'd rather work out barefoot and in jeans, and wear a wet, sweaty bra the rest of the day than return to my home and start the whole goodbye-scene again," she said.

As we all nodded in recognition, the talk turned to the vast panoply of lies, which go way beyond hiding out from your next of kin. When Daylight Savings Time came around, Ken and I didn't set the clock in the kids' room ahead, in the desperate hope they'd think it was 6 A.M.—not 7A.M.—and let us rest a little longer in the morning. Yes, we feel very guilty, but if it works, we're thinking of setting the clock back yet another hour. "Who knows where it will

From Here to Maternity

stop?" Ken asked. "If we get too greedy, it will be yesterday in their room."

And that's not the worst of it. They don't know the true ingredients of one of their favorite dishes. One night I made a smoked salmon and tomato omelet for me and Ken. Since my children won't accept a slice of pizza that's cut in the wrong way, I certainly wasn't about to serve them eggs and fish. "That's yuck," in toddler parlance. So we all sat down at the dinner table, and then, as if he'd been possessed by the spirit of a normal eater, my older son asked for a bite of the omelet. It wasn't "yuck." Ken and I wanted to cheer, but we kept our poker faces. The next thing we knew, his younger brother wanted a bite. "Here," the older boy said, spearing some omelet, "this is a piece of chicken, and here's some rice." "I like chicken and rice," my younger son said. No correction was uttered.

A few weeks later, I made the dish again. Like someone who can't bring herself to call her mother-in-law "Mom" or even use her first name—but who also knows "Mrs." is too formal—so ends up never calling her anything, I tried to avoid labeling. "What are we having for dinner?" my older son asked as I scrambled the eggs. "What you had the other night," I said. "What was it called?" he asked.

I hesitated as I thought of how important it is to set a good example, and how I want my children to grow up to be honest citizens, and I looked my son in the eyes and gave him the answer he knew to be right: "Chicken and rice."

Chapter 17

Got Milk Stains?

"Your People are calling," Ken said, without so much as a glance at the caller ID. He was right, of course. A major new-mom moment had just occurred at the Golden Globes, and there was urgent dishing to do.

Mary Louise Parker, three weeks post-partum, and buxom and gorgeous in a revealing black gown, had just won Best Supporting Actress for her portrayal of a drugged-out wife in *Angels in America*, and after thanking the usual suspects, she said, "Janel Moloney [Parker's colleague on *The West Wing*] said she would pay me a thousand dollars if I thanked my newborn son for my boobs looking so good in this dress. So, William Atticus Parker, thank you so much from your mother."

With the Hollywood audience laughing, Mary Louise looked out toward Moloney. "Get out your checkbook."

As everyone in the free world knew, Mary Louise had been dumped by the baby's dad, Billy Crudup, when she was seven months pregnant. And for Claire Danes—a younger woman, no less. This cast Mary Louise, momentarily, in the pitiable role of victim rather than enviable Hollywood star. "Good for her," I thought. Winning a Golden Globe, Mary Louise had triumphed over fickle jerks everywhere.

Forgetting for a moment that Mary Louise and I aren't really friends (though I am open to the idea), I was not only sharing in her joy but also fretting about the trouble she'll have taking care of a newborn on her own. A few days later, still thinking about her situation, I brought up the now-famous speech with Allison, which pitched her into a full-fledged screed.

"The whole moment struck me *not* because of her fabulous boobs," she said. "No, any new mom knows that comes with the territory. Temporarily. What shocked *me* was she had her child a week before and *didn't have on a bathrobe.* Her hair was—gasp!—*styled* and her dress was— gasp!—*probably a size two.* Plus she could form a *coherent sentence* and *smile.*"

My Mary Louise pity was beginning to ebb.

"It's bad enough that we women beat ourselves up because we don't walk around with Nicole Kidman's legs, Catherine Zeta-Jones's hair, and Halle Berry's flawless skin," she continued. "Now we're confronted with these impossibly toned, perky, well-rested Stepford Moms who gush about the glories of motherhood, and oh, the challenges.

Excuse me? Last I checked you had a nanny *or five*, and four assistant nannies, and could excuse yourself to the OTHER WING of the house when little Junior tested your nerves. And that's not counting the maids, gardeners, trainers, chefs, etcetera. I have to remind myself that I am *all of those things* and more—except maybe not the trainer, since I don't have time to work out!"

That's it! I thought—that's what makes motherhood so hard. It's Mary Louise—and Kate (Moss and Hudson), and Catherine and Brooke and Sarah Jessica and Elle and Madonna and Demi and Reese. If it weren't for them and their golden lives, I'd be breezing through these sleepless nights and two-berty tantrums. As if there weren't enough myths surrounding motherhood, the new wave of celebrity moms is here to provide constant (fake) living proof that maternal perfection is possible.

But enough with the jealous grumbling. We need an action plan. You know how Hollywood types are always fighting to improve conditions for garment workers in Thailand, or marching against fur, or going on fact-finding missions to war-torn lands, or testifying in front of Congress on the plight of farm workers? Well, how about if they were to speak up for yet another group of oppressed, or at least periodically depressed, people? What about a public service campaign—let's call it "Got Milk Stains?"—that would boost the self-esteem of new moms by making the celebrity moms look like regular people. The ads would counterbalance the seemingly endless assaults by tabloids and "Hollywood Minutes" and women's magazines, in which one celeb after another gushes about Life with Baby.*

I know what you Hollywood moms may be thinking: *What can I, just one megastar, possibly do to help?*

Here's what: Remember how Jamie Lee Curtis posed for *More* magazine sans makeup and flattering undergarments, to show the world what a real (real-ish, everything's relative) middle-aged woman looks like without the benefit of her stylist posse and flab wranglers? You could do something along the same lines. From reliable stories I read, Jamie Lee almost felt it was her duty as a forty-three-year-old woman to help Her People. "I don't have great thighs. I have very big breasts and a soft, fatty little tummy . . . It's insidious— glam Jamie, the perfect Jamie, the great figure, blah, blah, blah . . . It's such a fraud. And I'm the one perpetuating it."

So, all you celebrity moms out there, help stop the madness. Instead of publicly insisting that having a child has transformed you into this new wonderful person, and there's no one on earth you'd ever rather be with than your child, 24/7—Angelina!—how about using your acting skills

---

* Magazine editors may believe these articles are harmless, since new moms are known for having no time to read. But what editors may not realize is that while curling up with novels or keeping up on world events is impossible, the new mom's ability to devour any article on celebrity motherhood and pregnancy is actually *enhanced* (it's an evolutionary adaptation that makes a mother more "fit"). She might not recognize any books being reviewed in the *New York Times*, or know the names in Washington's latest political scandal, but she *will* know what a pregnant Cate Blanchett wore to an awards show.

to pretend you're an unkempt woman who loves her children but who needs a little break every now and then? Claim, if just for one *U.S. Weekly* interview, or a single *Entertainment Tonight* segment, that your back hurts from leaning over the diaper changing table and carrying your child. Say that you fired your nanny three weeks ago after you caught her watching TV while your kid sat crying alone in another room. Admit that you're at wit's end trying to find someone new, and not only that, but despite your personal chef and your trainer, you still can't lose the last ten pregnancy pounds.

I, for one, wouldn't mind seeing Kate Hudson, for instance, grocery shopping at 5:30 P.M. on a Friday. In exclusive supermarket surveillance footage, daytime TV watchers could thrill to scenes of Kate's son, Ryder, screaming to be lifted from the grocery cart and held while Kate tries to shop. We'd watch as she struggles to maneuver her cart among the throngs while holding her kicking child. Then, after getting less than half of what she came for, she makes an unfortunate choice of checkout lines. A very impatient Ryder is trying to pull down a rack of low-carb mini cookbooks and Kate's starting to lose it. Someone blocks the view momentarily, and all we see is Kate abandoning her cart and fleeing the store. And while Kate doesn't remember this, we all know there's nothing at home for the baby to eat, so she'll have to go back out again. At rush hour.

Now there's a Hollywood ending.

Or how about this: A *Vanity Fair* reporter is given access

to Michael Douglas and Catherine Zeta-Jones. The writer goes to their mansion prepared to write the usual celebrity puff piece, but something's amiss. The baby-sitter didn't show. Catherine's in the nursery changing Carys's dirty diaper, which grazes her Calvin Klein gown. The wipe only makes it worse. Working on her stain, she starts calling backup baby-sitters, but it's Oscar night so no one's available. Almost immediately, she and Michael start arguing over who gets to go to the Kodak Theater and do the Red Carpet thing, and who stays home with the kids. Neither gives in. They decide to bring the kids, so of course they're really late, but they might as well not have gone anyway, because the remaining time is spent in the theater's lobby dealing with two overtired children.

Other scenarios in the "Got Milk Stains?" campaign could involve a celebrity mom—Reese?—flying alone with an infant and preschooler, and struggling to install a car seat on the plane while trying to prevent her older child from running down the aisle. Or maybe Uma could be shown in the middle of a movie shoot when she gets The Call from her child's day care center reporting that the kid is running a fever and needs to be picked up immediately. "I adore my children," participating celeb Madonna would whisper as she covers Rocco's or Lourdes's ears, "but even with three nannies I get tired sometimes. I just want to spend one night alone in a hotel room, and go to the bathroom without someone hanging all over me."

While I'm casting and producing, I'll make some wardrobe changes, too. I'm not suggesting that Hollywood moms in the campaign need dress like slobs, but instead of going out dressed in Celeb Casual—designer sneakers, Seven jeans, Prada T-shirt—let's do dingy New Balance running shoes, sweatpants with the knees bagging out, a shapeless cotton sweater, and—this is crucial—no showering for three days before any public appearance. Courtney Cox, we're ready for your close-up.

But as tempting as it is to place all the blame on celebrities, they're only part of our problem, and as such can only be part of the solution. We also need help from the hardworking journalists. We know that stories about stars smoking, binge drinking, or looking rail-thin send a dangerous message to an impressionable audience. But what about the relentless focus on babies as the latest Hollywood "accessory"?

Who knows how many childless women who are on the fence about having kids—but who are definitely in favor of accessories—might read a cutesy headline and think, *Oh what the heck, I could use something to dress up that little black dress of mine, I'll have a baby.* The way the stories are written, a woman in her childbearing years could almost find herself searching a magazine's "Where to Buy It" section to see who sells those adorable little baby numbers. *Hmm, dark hair or light, which would go better with me?*

The next thing she knows, she's got her must-have item—and with only a nine-month wait, about a third of the time it takes for your Hermes Birkin bag to arrive. But what does she find? Rather than dress up an outfit, or take a look from day to night, this accessory destroys ensembles and dashes any hope of sleep. As *Sesame Street* would put it, "One of these accessories is not like the others"—or in *Sesame Street*'s later, PC parlance, "One of these accessories is doing its own thing." Such as: running around a restaurant pulling down tablecloths and zipping through the swinging kitchen doors, or wrinkling the very simple dress it was supposed to enliven.

I was complaining about this bait-and-switch being perpetrated on American women when Dana, a woman who knows her accessories, told me I misunderstood just how the baby as *object* should be used. "These are not accessories you wear or keep anywhere near your person when you're out in public," she explained. "They're a sign of affluence, but they are rarely seen. It is known that you have two children of your own, and seven more whom you've adopted. The child's like a DeSoto that's only taken out on a perfect day—and then for only twenty minutes before being driven back into the baby garage to be tended by its mechanic."

One can only imagine the stress the celebrity infant must feel to coo on cue, or to always look adorable, or to endure life with Glinda Nirvana Pineapple Star for a name. And really, who wants a mom with skin softer than your own? If all that's not bad enough, the pressure to hang for hours in that Baby Bjorn, just for the obligatory casual-movie-star-parents-walking-on-Melrose photo op, must be intense.

Got Milk Stains?

And let's talk about one more group affected by this "celebration" of motherhood: pregnant women. In the old days, pregnancy was a nine-month break from sartorial concerns, but no longer. Thanks to all these high-profile pregnancies and the attendant boom in designer maternity clothes—at Target prices, no less—expectant women are now supposed to look sexy. I was lunching with Helen when she was almost nine months along with her second child, and, as fashion dictated, she was wearing a belly-hugging top and cropped pants, the better to showcase her swollen ankles, and during her second trip to the ladies' room she called me at the table from her cell phone. "Can you go out and buy me a change of clothes *right now*?" she whispered, having just caught sight of herself in the mirror. "I feel so ridiculous. I don't dress like this when I'm not pregnant, why now?"

Because *InStyle* said so, that's why.

So celebrities, I'm begging you, give the rest of us a chance to shine. As Allison put it, "Madonna's already been everything I wanted to be from high school on. I could never be the Material Girl or Evita, but I could be—I am—a mother. Did she have to co-opt that, too?"

I understood Allison's feelings, and yet as she spoke, I couldn't help but wonder if perhaps, dear reader, the fault lies not with our stars, but with ourselves.

Actually, I *could* help it. It's all their fault.

Chapter 18

Happy Mother's Day or:
How I Learned to Stop Worrying
and Love Two-berty

"When did you become a mother?"

The question stopped me cold, although that was hardly the intention.

I was rushing home from work, pushing to make my child care deadline (which is more stressful than any newspaper deadline I've ever faced), when I ran into a former colleague. We hadn't seen each other in ten years, but we took up right where we'd left off, gossiping about editors and griping about assignments, like true journalists. I was dying to grab an outdoor table at the nearby Armani café and spend the evening sipping Shiraz and wearing sunglasses way past when they're necessary, but there was the small matter of the clock. "I'm so sorry," I said as she launched into what promised to be a delicious but lengthy anecdote, "but my nanny leaves at five."

"You have a child?" she said. "When did you become a mother?"

"Child*ren*," I said. "I have two kids. Boys."

But even as I was setting the record straight, I was grappling with her second question: When *did* I become a mother?

Technically? The day my first son was born. But you know how referring to your brand-new husband as "my husband" makes you feel like a stranger to yourself, even though others seem to think it's perfectly normal? The same holds true for being a mom. Almost immediately after giving birth, I noticed a disconnect between the way the rest of the world perceived me, as a you-know-what, and the way I thought of myself: as a baby-sitter, infatuated with her charge, but nonetheless waiting for the parents to return.

Admittedly, the evidence—in addition to the actual baby—proved beyond any doubt that I was a mother. If I were merely baby-sitting, there was going to be some explaining to do to the *Herald*'s human resources department—maternity leave ain't cheap. Plus, I was spending a lot of time stooped at a very uncomfortable angle, swinging a crying infant in his car seat, and who but a parent would risk an almost certain lower-back injury just to stop a little wailing?

I think I had trouble internalizing my new title because

the whole thing had been so sudden. Sure I'd had nine months to prepare, but I was working on the pregnant-woman thing then, not motherhood. In other areas of life, you ramp up in responsibility. You're not employed as a nurse's aide one day and a brain surgeon the next, with everyone running around calling you "doctor" and deferring to your expertise.

But standing there on the street that day, talking to my former colleague—an unmarried newshound whose quandaries did not include whether to take the kids grocery shopping before work, an exhausting proposition, or go alone in the evening, thereby blowing her one hour of free time—I decided a simple answer would be best. "My older son's already three," I said. "I've been a mom for a while."

"That's great," she said. "Look, I know you have to run, but let's get drinks sometime soon?"

"Yes, let's," I said, but I knew it would be years before I'd score a cocktail pass at bath time. Continuing on my way, I thought about how I'd felt like such a mom temp in those early months—and not even a good one. But here's the thing about Temporary—it's just Permanent being naïve. The blanket thrown over the new chair "just until" Rover learns to stay off the furniture is still there the day you move (and Rover has long since moved on to greener pastures). The magazines placed on your nightstand form a second tabletop. It's like that with work, too. One day you're wearing a VISITOR sticker and not bothering to learn the phone system because you know you'll be leaving to start your real career in a few days, and then suddenly you're the one showing the new woman where the cafeteria is and referring to the company as "we."

When did I make the big switch, from baby-sitter to mommy, from Kelly Girl to veteran? Like being well-read or having a fabulous antique-plate collection, it's not the kind of thing that happens overnight. What I do know is this: somewhere between my older son's two-week pediatrician's appointment—when he was crying in his stroller as I read the *New York Times*, sitting right next to him but oblivious to his discomfort—and a Saturday afternoon earlier this month, when *I* was the mom at the birthday party who lent an emergency change of clothes to a small guest who suffered a toilet training accident, it happened to me: I started to feel like the real deal.

Where once I told everyone I met in the park or at new-moms' groups that I worked at the *Herald*, and was constantly trying to maneuver conversations around to real-world events (and away from teething and dirty diaper talk), I started to find myself initiating stroller discussions and dropping references to my children at work—and not just to explain why I had crayon on my shirt, either. Even more telling, my definition of news changed from, let's say, the discovery of evidence that there had once been liquid water on Mars, to the fact that I'd found replacement valves for the Playtex sippy cups on the Internet. "Ken, Drugstore.com has them!" I practically shouted into his answering machine.

And there is another, perhaps more significant sign. I've started talking to babies who aren't mine. I'll be on line at the grocery store and I'll spot a baby nearby. Whereas in the past I might have given the mother a polite smile and returned to reading the tabloid borrowed from the rack, I now actively engage the infant. "Where'd you get those big blue eyes?" I might say. "Does your mommy know how cute you are?" I start games of peek-a-boo.

When my older son was a little baby, I myself had been thrown into a panic when friendly women started conversations with him. *What should I do?* I always wondered. Throw my voice and speak in a falsetto as if I were him? Speak through him, keeping up the fiction that he was the one in the conversation? "Tell the nice lady you're seven months old."

Here's another way I know I'm a mom: if you tell a person without kids an anecdote about your children, she'll tell you one about herself as a child. Not only have I stopped passing along tales of my girlhood, but the other day I heard myself regaling (torturing?) a young editorial assistant at work with a cute story about how my kids kiss each other good-bye when they're parting in the morning, like lovers at a train station, and how they like to sit facing each other on the couch, the soles of their feet touching. "And you should see them crossing the street holding hands," I called out, as she disappeared into the ladies' room.

Goldie Hawn—before she became a grandmother—observed that there are three ages of women in Hollywood:

babe, district attorney, and *Driving Miss Daisy*. Goldie doesn't have a similar axiom for the ages of motherhood, and none of the parenting books spell out Mommy's Developmental Milestones, but the more I tried to nail down my metamorphosis, the more I realized that motherhood has identifiable stages, too ("babe" not among them):

1) *Infancy*. The mother can do almost nothing for herself, not bathe, chat on the phone, check e-mail, shop, or go to Pilates. During this period meltdowns, fussiness, and imaginary friends (friends who were once real, but who are now only a presence on the phone, if that) are common.

2) *Ziplock baggies*. The mother travels everywhere with three or four pounds of Cheerios, Goldfish, halved grapes, cheese sticks, fruit leather, peanut butter sandwiches, Pirate's Booty, and sippy cups. Having shed her stranger anxiety, the mother often arranges playdates, but rather than interact with the other mom, as hoped, frequent interruptions cause the two mommies to engage in "parallel play."

3) *"Your foot does not belong in the refrigerator."* This stage is marked by an increase in "I'm turning into my mother" statements that, once shocking to the mom uttering them, no longer surprise her. These include such favorites as "If you can't share it I'm throwing it away" and "Please take your strawberry off your brother's head," which someone in my home—me?—said the other day.

4) *Mrs. Kravitz.* Named for the nosy neighbor on *Bewitched*, this stage starts the moment a mother decides she has expertise that others need, and feels free to offer advice to complete strangers. Her passed-along wisdom includes admonitions such as "Put a hat on that child," "He's getting too much sun," and "You should Purell his hands before you let him eat after playing in the sandbox."

5) *Ma Bell.* A mother in this phase believes that anyone who calls her home—colleagues, the plumber, people on cell phones almost out of minutes—want nothing more than to carry on one-way conversations with a small child. As the kid utters "Yes" and "No" answers, the mother in the throes of Ma Bell stands by beaming with pride. The Ma Bell ma also thinks it's cute to have her child—preverbal though he may be—record the outgoing message on her answering machine.

I was at the park with Helen, still trying to pinpoint when I became a real mom, when she threw another question my way: "When do you most *feel* like a mom?"

I opened a ziplock baggie and started to work my way through the halved grapes I'd packed for my sons. "That's an interesting question," I said, taking out some Pirate's Booty and glancing over to the sandbox to make sure my kids were still there. Because my mother and father and brother and I have so much fun together, I'd always associated parenthood with joy. Somehow I didn't realize the job had its share of drudgery, nor did I think about the fact that mastering the daughter role in no way meant I'd ace motherhood.

"I feel like a mom when I'm having a nice time with them and, in turn, I think they're enjoying my company," I said. I was thinking about the day the kids and I hung out on the street corner watching a backhoe dig into the middle of the road, and a night not long ago when my older son said he wanted to tell me a bedtime story, and began, "Once upon a time there was a woman named Mommy, and she was the best astronaut in the whole country." And the day when my younger son was home sick, he and I were singing "Puff the Magic Dragon" along with Peter, Paul and Mary and swinging our heads to the music, and he said he wanted long hair "like Mommy's."

I rooted around in my knapsack for some seltzer water, and realizing I'd left the bottle in the car, surreptitiously took a swig from a sippy cup. "But it's not just when we're having fun," I said, "but when I realize how much they need me." I thought back to the wonderful nurse who'd taught the parenting course I took during my first pregnancy. "The one thing you can't forget," she'd said, "is that *you* are that baby's mother. No one else. *You.* You are responsible for that child. No one else will care as much about him or her as you do. He's yours."

It was scary stuff, but heady, too. I think of that nurse when one of my boys wakes up with a bad dream and instinctively calls "Mommy," and I realize that although I can't make a decent Halloween costume, I can help my boys feel safe and happy. Her words were ringing in my ears the day I cut short an important meeting because I couldn't reach the brand-new baby-sitter on her cell phone. The cloudy day had turned sunny, and I feared she hadn't brought sunblock to the park (she hadn't).

Somewhere between the fun of hanging out at construction sites and the maternal satisfaction of comforting a child, there's daily life, with its challenges of two-berty* but also increasing pleasures. A few days ago I took the kids grocery shopping before school. We debated which store to hit—escalator versus child-sized carts—and then took off for Whole Foods (pricey, but with transportation on its side).

We formed a tiny convoy to the fruit section. We were almost at the watermelon when my younger son got his cart tangled up with an organic goat cheese display. "Walk backwards and pull your cart," my older son said, going to his brother's rescue. The three of us were cracking up—is anything as beautiful as the sound of a preschooler's belly laugh?—when another shopper smiled at me. "You're a stronger woman than I am," she said.

I could tell by the way she said it that she'd had some bad shopping experiences, and because I had too, I smiled back. "Believe me," I said, "it's not what it looks like."

---

* Two-berty, as I've mentioned, is the toddle-version of adolescence. The two-bertal child is every bit as hormonal, rebellious, and unpredictable as a pubertal thirteen-year-old.

Or was it?

Yesterday morning I overheard my kids chatting in their bedroom at 5:30. "Is Mommy awake?" my younger son asked his brother. "Can you see her?"

Wow, I thought, sort of wishing they were still asleep, but loving their conversation, *that's me they're talking about.* I *am Mommy*.

Acknowledgments

*W*hy did I *really* write this book? In hopes of getting some rest. Yeah, coming up with almost two hundred pages of material was a ton of work, but when you've got two young children who wake several times a night—each—the idea of a book tour was, how shall I say, attractive.

The only question was what to write about (a small matter, but one that did need to be settled). I'll be forever grateful to my mother-in-law, Bette Mandl, and my friend Carey Goldberg for coming up with the perfect topic.

I consider myself beyond lucky to have Brettne Bloom, of Kneerim & Williams, as my agent and Ann Campbell, at Broadway Books, as my editor. Their hard work and terrific enthusiasm greatly enriched this book. Much gratitude also to Ursula Cary, Laura Pillar, Julia Coblentz, David Drake, Heather McGuire, Catherine Pollock, Umi Kenyon, and the rest of the incredible team at Broadway.

My editors at the *Boston Herald* were more than generous in giving me time to write this book, and then more than generous in their suggestions as to how it could be improved. Linda Kincaid and Sande Kent, thank you for your wit and support. My *Herald* colleagues Gustavo Leon, Kathy Geosites Howlett, Tara Bricking, and Susan Pearson were also hugely helpful, and I'm grateful for their time and flair. I was also fortunate to have the help of the talented Devra Ehrenberg and the wise Jim Behrle.

Michael J. Rosen, thanks for the best correspondence humor-writing course anyone's ever taught. I'm sorry about the fax machine. And Marie Morris, you rule—and tighten and brighten.

I couldn't have written this book without the laughter and friendship (and anecdotes) of the following people: Kim Ambach, Jenny Clancy, Shelagh Collins, Shep Doeleman, Jane Dornbusch, Lauren Beckham Falcone, Emily Gelbert, Lisa Jacobs, Robin Jalajas, Emily Kuvin, Susan McConathy, Amy Morgan, Jennifer Ovelette, Jill Radsken, Daphne Santana, Jan Saragoni, Susan Senator, Emily Terry, and Elissa Weitzman.

Mark and Linda Teitell were a steady source of encouragement, and always happy to tell me one more time that "it gets easier"—the child-rearing, not the writing. With their regular Sunday afternoon baby-sitting gig, and joyful loving presence, my in-laws, Bette and Alex Mandl, really made this project possible. And Mom and Dad, what's there to say?

And finally, a minivan-sized thanks to Ken, my husband/editor/agent/coach/gag writer/person who reminded me of all the funny things I'd forgotten about along the way, and who gently recommended—oh, so many times—that I carry a small notebook and jot things down. See, I remembered.